DUAL LANGUAGE ED
FOR A
TRANSFORMED WORLD

Wayne P. Thomas and Virginia P. Collier

DUAL LANGUAGE EDUCATION OF NEW MEXICO

ALBUQUERQUE, NM   FUENTE PRESS   **FUENTE PRESS**

Dual Language Education of New Mexico
Fuente Press

1309 Fourth St. SW, Suite E
Albuquerque, NM 87102
www.dlenm.org

©2012 by Wayne P. Thomas and Virginia P. Collier

All rights reserved. No part of this book may be reproduced in any form or by any electronic or mechanical means, including information storage and retrieval systems, without permission in writing from the publisher, except by a reviewer, who may quote brief passages in a review, with the exception of reproducible figures, which are identified by the *Thomas and Collier* copyright line and can be photocopied for educational use only.

Library of Congress Control Number: 2012950476

ISBN 978-0-9843169-1-5

DEDICATION

To dual language educators everywhere,

transforming learning

throughout the world:

Our time has come!

TABLE OF CONTENTS

ACKNOWLEDGMENTS

Again, we are ever so grateful to the staff of Dual Language Education of New Mexico for the immense collaborative effort to publish this second in a planned series of books. Dee McMann, Materials Development Coordinator, and David Rogers, Executive Director of DLeNM, took the lead roles of reading and responding in depth to this manuscript, making invaluable suggestions for editing and strengthening the points made throughout this book. Dee's and David's experience and expertise in the field of dual language education is present throughout the text, including when the research findings implied differences with practitioners' perspectives.

We are also extremely grateful to the dual language educators in North Carolina, Texas, Maine, and Oregon who have welcomed us to conduct research and have dedicated their professional lives to transforming their educational contexts so that all students can thrive. These communities have opened their doors to new ways of enhancing schools so that everyone benefits. Thanks to you dedicated educators for letting us share your story.

We also acknowledge the 25 years of support and the enabling spirits of our colleagues at George Mason University. We are honored by our appointments as emeritus professors, and look forward to many years of continued connections. And most of all, great thanks go to our families and friends sharing the journey with us – especially our Unity and Cinema friends in central Virginia. You have continued to provide inspiration that helps us visualize and co-create a transformed world for all.

PREFACE

Ginger's story

It was 1971. My oldest daughter, a second grader, had just enrolled in a new Spanish-English bilingual class at our neighborhood public school in Washington, D.C. How did this happen to us, and what would it mean for my precious seven-year-old?

With increasing numbers of Latino immigrants arriving in the city each year since the early 1960s, cultural clashes had erupted between African American and Latino students. African Americans (73% of the city's population) dominated local politics and school administration, whereas Latinos were a small but growing minority at 7%. After experiencing many frustrations, the D.C. Latino community authored a grant with which they funded coursework to certify the first Spanish-speaking teachers and counselors to be hired to provide instruction and guidance in Spanish for the Latino students in the school system. The bilingual program that emerged was based on the two-way model being implemented in Florida and Massachusetts at that time. The bilingual classes would serve both Spanish- and English-speaking students, with an emphasis on an equal exchange of ideas, use of two languages, and learning experiences through the intermixing of all cultural groups who chose to participate. We were early implementers and pioneers of a growing community of educators that would advocate for and launch over 800 dual language programs across the United States over the next four decades.

So here I was, an anxious parent, wondering how well this small experiment was going to turn out. The school had a balanced mixture of African American, White, and Latino students across a range of income levels. The community was very committed to inner-city living and the public school system, and many parents were involved in resolution of a variety of social justice issues within their city and schools.

The bilingual program director chose to assign a pair of teachers to my daughter's combined first- and second-grade classroom. Pretty soon I knew these two women well, because I couldn't stay out of their classroom—it was so fascinating to watch what developed! Sherry Shumavon, the English-medium teacher of this team, had previously team taught in bilingual classes in California and was familiar with this two-way innovation. Eliana Román, the Spanish-medium teacher, had been trained in the Chilean teacher education system, focused on discovery learning, that had been developed by the famous poet Gabriela Mistral. As a result, she brought a new dimension to the school, mentoring other teachers and creatively mixing age groups throughout the school for varied cross-cultural activities.

The two bilingual teachers were very compatible, and they showered students with love throughout each day. The educational activities were hands-on and child-centered—geometry through origami and string designs, conceptual math with geoboards and cocoa beans and varied counting items, science through cooking experiments and growing plants, animals for keeping journals and re-

cords, canciones y ritmos on the playground with jumping ropes and varied ball games, students and teachers singing songs from Latin America and the U.S. as they worked on projects. Once students made the leaps into reading and writing in both target languages, their individual journals in Spanish and English demonstrated remarkable progress during the year. It was magical! *El chisme bilingüe/Bilingual Gossip* became a monthly journal that the students published in both languages, with their poems and stories and accompanying artwork. *Cuentos* (stories) around Sra. Román's rocking chair with puppets and
realia (items from everyday life) evolved into cross-cultural sharing and comparing. Social studies projects included mapping and analyzing the neighborhood sociologically. Parents contributed cross-cultural experiences and many after-school events deepened the relationships that developed among the families of our students.

What an introduction to bilingual schooling I had as a parent in my daughter's school! Ironically, it had not occurred to me to raise my children bilingually, even though I had grown up naturally acquiring Spanish in my childhood from several year-long trips to Central America by car when my dad, a Latin American history professor, was collecting information for his books. So this experience as a parent led me to courses on Spanish and English linguistics and bilingualism and second language acquisition, becoming a bilingual/ESL middle school teacher with a specialty in social studies, and eventually pursuing my Ph.D. in intercultural education. And here I am 40 years later, continuing to verify through our Thomas and

Collier research that this form of schooling is unique in assisting all students to get truly excited about school and to succeed academically, cognitively, linguistically, socioculturally— and to achieve higher than in traditional monolingual education settings!

Wayne's story

I first met Dr. Collier in the fall of 1980, as we new faculty in the School of Education at George Mason University were getting acquainted. As she discussed bilingual education, I thought, quite frankly, that she was crazy. I had never heard of such an innovation before, and based on "common sense," I was quite sure that it would not work well. After all, I thought, how could those students possibly do better in school when receiving less than full-time instruction in English? While I had studied three other languages as subjects in high school and at university, I had grown up in a monolingual English environment in Virginia. My immigrant ancestors in the early 1700s had spoken Gaelic, Scots, Welsh, and German, but I was personally unfamiliar with the immigrant experience in the U.S. Even my Cherokee great-grandmother had merged into the White world and did not pass on her heritage to my generation.

In my prior work in schools as a teacher and administrator, I had focused on social justice issues through evaluating and improving Title I programs for low-income Whites and Blacks, and I was quite concerned about assisting students who were most at risk. Dr. Collier described the challenges that immigrant students faced in school, the importance of keeping these students on grade level while they acquired English, and how this could best be done through schooling in both their native language and English. I proposed that, even though I remained a skeptic about bilingual schooling, as a specialist in research and program evaluation methodology I could be convinced by data. That led to our first collaborative research study in a large school district.

We chose a school district in which the administration wanted us to analyze their data on immigrant students. They had an outstanding ESL program with small class sizes and committed ESL teachers who worked hard to serve the students well. The students were mostly of Asian-language background and were doing well in school, according to the grades they received from teachers. But when we analyzed their scores on standardized norm-referenced tests, we found that they were not scoring at all well on the language measures, even after many years of schooling in the United States. That was our first shocking discovery of how long it seems to take to get to grade level in second language and what factors influence immigrants' school success. In our study, the variable that most strongly influenced success in English was how much formal schooling these students had received in their home country and in their home language before arriving in the U.S., NOT how much proficiency in English they had achieved.

This was an eye-opener for Dr. Collier, but it represented an attitudinal sea-change for me. I realized that this group of students—even larger than the Title I and special education populations—was also the fastest growing population in U.S. schools and the least funded by federal and state agencies. Understanding that the social justice issues of culturally and linguistically diverse students were just as important as those of the Title I population, I resolved to make this field a major part of my future professional work as a university professor. And so our collaboration began.

Wayne's and Ginger's joint story

As we continued with further studies, we became well known for the "how long" questions that we asked of longitudinal data and the variables that influence how long it takes English learners to reach grade-level achievement in English. Figure 5.2 from our first book in this series (Collier & Thomas, 2009) is known and used world-wide, and many refer to it as "the six-lined graph" or simply "The Graph." We are reprinting it in Chapter Six of this book (see Figure 6.1) so that you know what we're referring to. Researchers in all continents of the world have confirmed that they have found similar patterns in their data when they follow students longitudinally.

From all of our studies to date, the bottom line is this: when students receive schooling through their primary language and the second language all the way through the first six years of schooling, with at least half of the instructional time in their primary language, they can reach grade level in second language and stay there through the remainder of their schooling. If they get continuing support through their primary language into the middle school and high school years, they can reach even higher than grade-level achievement in second language. Furthermore, when they graduate from high school bilingual/biliterate/bicultural, they are prepared to fully participate in a global world of the 21st century.

We feel extremely privileged to be in a position to bring these clear research findings to countries around the world. With over six million student records that we have now analyzed from all regions of the United States, our conclusions are fully validated. This model of schooling through two languages that we have found to be most effective is what this book is all about. We are using the term "dual language education" as the most commonly used label for this type of enrichment schooling. In the first chapters of this book, we review the important characteristics of this model that the research shows make a difference in effectiveness. The remaining chapters focus on our research findings to date.

May you enjoy your journey with us in reading this book, as well as the first book on which it is based—*Educating English Learners for a Transformed World* (Collier & Thomas, 2009). We look forward to your present and future collaboration with other dual language educators who are creating thriving multilingual/multicultural classroom environments in schools across the U.S. and around the world. You will be educating all children for the highly diverse and interactive world of the 2030s and beyond, and there is no more important task for the benefit of all of us. You can leave no better legacy to the future than your professional and personal success in doing so.

Wayne and Ginger

OVERVIEW OF THE BOOK

This second book is a continuation of our first book published with Dual Language Education of New Mexico's Fuente Press, *Educating English Learners for a Transformed World* (Collier & Thomas, 2009). In this book, we are focusing on the enrichment form of bilingual schooling that U.S. educators now call "dual language education." This program model is for all students, unlike traditional forms of bilingual instruction in the U.S. designed only for English learners. We discuss the most important defining characteristics of dual language education that research has shown to greatly improve education, and we demonstrate the power of this program model through our most recent research findings.

Our first chapter, *Reasons to Consider Dual Language Programs*, is purposefully short, to be used as a condensed summary of the benefits of dual language education and the major research findings on dual language programs reported throughout the book. In this first chapter, we do not cite references in order not to interrupt the points being made, but the references are presented in the more detailed text of the chapters that follow. Almost all of these findings in the first chapter are from our own work and that of Kathryn Lindholm-Leary, who has spent her professional lifetime conducting evaluation research on dual language programs in the U.S. For parents, educators, and policy makers who want to convince others to implement or expand dual language programs, this chapter is written for you!

Chapter Two, *Beginnings*, chronicles the history of bilingual schooling in the U.S. from which dual language education developed. This chapter provides important background regarding the relationship between the various program models that were developed for English learners as well as bilingual programs designed for native English speakers. We introduce program labels and terms used for dual language, contrasting these with subtractive models developed for English learners that have been shown to be much less effective than additive dual language programs. Dr. Collier (Ginger) lived this history and has served as one of the historians of our field as it has developed in the U.S. from the 1960s to the present.

The third and fourth chapters focus on the non-negotiable characteristics and qualities that make dual language programs work so effectively. Chapter Three, *Defining Dual Language Education*, discusses both two-way and one-way models, showing that both are equally effective enrichment models. Also defined are differences between 90:10 and 50:50 programs, with our research showing that 90:10 is the most efficient in getting English learners to grade-level in their second language, even though this involves less instructional time in English initially. We also introduce the non-negotiables of dual language schooling in detail: K-12 commitment, separation of the two languages, and at least 50% of the curriculum taught through the partner language. Chapter Four, *Unique Qualities of Dual Language Education*, discusses additional implementation decisions, including who will participate in the program, recruitment of teachers and staff, instructional practices, and community engagement.

The fifth and sixth chapters provide new Thomas and Collier research findings on dual language education that have not been published to date. The North Carolina research reported in Chapter Five, *Astounding Effectiveness: The North Carolina Story*, is quite an amazing story, with dual language education serving as a very positive influence on student achievement for all student groups, including English learners, Latinos, African Americans, Caucasian Americans, students of low-income background, and students with special needs. Chapter Six, *More Dual Language Research Findings from Thomas and Collier*, includes findings from our research in Woodburn, Oregon, on dual language schools as well as key points regarding a summary of all our research, as reflected in the Thomas and Collier research figure that is most popular.

Chapter Seven, *The Beauty of Dual Language Education*, summarizes why dual language education is so successful. For those who are not yet convinced, this is another chapter worth reading. Dual language education is based on well-defined theory, is maximally effective with all groups of students, and is politically attractive because it is integrative and inclusive. This vehicle for school reform works well and provides important benefits for everyone—students, educators, families, and the community. We hope you enjoy your reading!

DUAL LANGUAGE EDUCATION
FOR A
TRANSFORMED WORLD

Wayne P. Thomas and Virginia P. Collier

DUAL LANGUAGE EDUCATION OF NEW MEXICO

ALBUQUERQUE, NM   FUENTE PRESS   **FUENTE PRESS**

REFLECTIONS FROM THE FIELD

"...and justice for all"...Something heard every day in the hallways of our schools across this country, yet still remaining to be seen. Equity-minded, visionary schools and districts dare to believe that justice for all can and should be their primary focus, and consequently adopt board policies that make equity and access a priority. Then they walk the talk, recognizing that their culturally and linguistically diverse populations create a golden opportunity to promote equity and equity-mindedness for all involved. They understand that gap closure is best accomplished through directly and unapologetically addressing the linguistic and cultural needs of their student populations.

For more than 25 years, the equity-minded, visionary research of Wayne Thomas and Virginia Collier has confirmed that well-implemented two-way bilingual immersion programs are the optimal program to close the achievement gap for English learners, and this research has been the driving force for the adoption of two-way bilingual immersion programs around the country. Their research and undying commitment to sharing the message has indeed inspired schools and districts to dare to believe that we can, one classroom at a time, move closer to the goal of justice for all.

MICHELE ANBERG-ESPINOSA, ED.D.

WORLD LANGUAGE/DUAL LANGUAGE PROGRAM ADMINISTRATOR
SAN FRANCISCO UNIFIED SCHOOL DISTRICT, CALIFORNIA

CHAPTER ONE: REASONS TO CONSIDER DUAL LANGUAGE PROGRAMS

Educators who have worked in the field of language education know that there are many reasons to study languages. In the traditional curriculum for U.S. schools, English language arts teachers offer required courses for all the Grades K-12, while foreign language teachers provide courses in other languages as an elective at middle and high school levels. These courses analyze the language being studied and its use in varied contexts (usually literature).

But dual language is really different! In a dual language program, the two languages are acquired through all the subjects of the curriculum. And this program is potentially for all students. Dual language classes deepen the students' and teachers' collaborative content explorations, using at least two languages as the vehicle for all curricular studies. The understanding is that teachers and students will work to meet or exceed the academic standards of math, science, social studies, and language arts for each grade level. Simultaneously, students are acquiring deeper and deeper ability to use the two program languages in oral and written form, eventually reaching native-like speaker proficiency in English and at least one other language. In other words, using the school's core curriculum is a powerful way to naturally acquire a second language while fully developing the native language.

The benefits don't stop there. Learning through two languages expands and enhances students' thinking skills, ensuring that students' cognitive development and flexibility surpass that achieved through a curriculum delivered in only one language. On top of that, students from diverse backgrounds learn to respect and value each other as partners in the learning/acquiring process.

So what does the research tell us?

When comparing dual language (DL) classrooms to English as a second language (ESL) or to mainstream English classrooms:

- English learners in DL score very significantly higher on state tests as well as norm-referenced tests than in ESL-only programs.

- English learners in DL master much more of the curriculum, academically and linguistically, than English learners in ESL-only programs. They experience full gap closure rather than partial gap closure.

- English learners in DL master English better than English learners in ESL-only programs (even though only half or less than half of their instruction is in English).

- Language minority students who are fluent in English and of the same heritage as the English learners can enroll in DL classes (whereas they are not served in transitional bilingual or ESL-only classes). In DL classes, these students score higher on state tests as well as norm-referenced tests than language minority students in the English mainstream classroom.

- African American native English speakers in DL score very significantly higher on state tests as well as norm-referenced tests than African American students in the English mainstream classroom.

- White native English speakers in DL score higher on state tests as well as norm referenced tests than White native English speakers in the English mainstream classroom.

- Title I-eligible students in DL score significantly higher on state tests as well as norm-referenced tests than Title I-eligible students in the English mainstream classroom.

- Special needs students in DL score higher on state tests than special needs students in the English mainstream classroom.

- DL students don't just study a second language as a subject (as is typical in foreign language classes); they become fully proficient in a second language at no cost to their English development.

- DL students have more favorable attitudes toward being bilingual and toward students who are different from themselves than do students in the English mainstream classroom.

- DL students report high levels of satisfaction and enjoyment in DL classes.

- DL students have stronger cultural identity and high self-esteem.

- Student engagement with instruction is higher in DL classes.

- Student overall interest in school is higher in DL programs.

- Student overall attendance is better in DL programs.

- Significantly fewer behavioral referrals are experienced in DL classes than in the English mainstream classes.

- Costs for DL are less than for ESL-only because DL is a mainstream (not a separate remedial) program that is taught through two (rather than one) languages. Some extra costs may be needed for second language materials, but no additional classroom teachers are needed as in ESL-only and transitional bilingual education pullout classes.

- In DL classrooms, required teaching strategies (e.g., cooperative learning, with emphasis on grade-level cognitive, linguistic, and academic development in a favorable sociocultural school setting) lead to more effective, efficient, and productive instruction using the same amount of instructional time as mainstream English classrooms.

- In two-way (two language groups being schooled through their two languages) DL classrooms, instructional interaction with same-age peers (and peer language models) provides the ideal context for the enhancement of natural second language acquisition.

- Learning in two languages develops unactivated brain areas and increases creativity and problem-solving skills.

And that's not all! Dual language programs have a positive influence on all those who participate in or interact with the education system—especially parents, administrators, teachers, and students.

Parents. Parents must grow with the dual language program. They must be one of the first groups exposed to the research and rationale for dual language education for students from all linguistic backgrounds. As they come to understand the process (language acquisition, learning in two languages, etc.) their children are going through, their initial anxieties diminish and they frequently become the program's greatest advocates. The bilingual/bicultural context of a well-implemented dual language program nurtures everyone. The school may provide cross-cultural events for families, including exchanges of skills and shared language learning experiences. Parents from all walks of life can come together in support of their children and their school's programs. Parent meetings focus on the needs of their multilingual/multicultural community.

As families come to value their neighborhood dual language school, they work harder to find ways to stay, so historically high mobility rates are lowered. Families are committed to their children remaining at the school for as many grades as possible, lessening attrition, which is a common concern in schools that serve low-income neighborhoods. A committed group of parents who understand the program well can explain the concepts of linguistic, academic, cognitive, and sociocultural development through two languages to the newly arriving families who may initially be skeptical of such a complex program. Common questions of new parents can be confidently answered by the more experienced parents in dual language programs. The parents' ability to explain how dual language education works is the most powerful form of advocacy that a parent can engage in.

With a well-implemented dual language program in place, both English-speaking parents and the parents who speak the other program language become advocates for bilingualism in the community. A core of committed parents can stem the political forces that might question the value of bilingualism, locally or even statewide. Funding appropriations for dual language schools and policies that promote bilingualism and biliteracy for all citizens are outcomes advocated by parents committed to schooling their children through two languages. Dual language parents shape the future by reinforcing the intercultural values of our society and encouraging their multilingual children to be internationally collaborative adults for the mid-21st century.

Administrators. Principals of well-implemented dual language schools truly love what they do. Those who have created a schoolwide dual language program tend to stay in these positions for many years; it can be hard to persuade a dual language principal to retire. The commitment to the community and the satisfaction of creating a bilingual/bicultural gathering place is more than enough reason to remain. Principals become re-energized when they see the higher student attainment as well as increased collaboration among students of diverse backgrounds in their schools.

As with any new program, first year implementation of dual language is usually challenging. It is the responsibility of the principal to deeply understand the dual language program, to build teacher and parent support, and to provide intensive staff development and instructional coaching support. After recruiting the first bilingual teachers who will partner with the English-speaking staff, the principal must be constantly on the lookout for teachers truly proficient in the partner language as the program grows grade by grade. This takes patience, confidence, and a strategic staffing recruitment plan.

During the start-up years, extra funds are often sought to purchase curricular materials in both languages and to provide extra staff development for teachers. Seeking grant funds and community business partners can be a joint responsibility of the central office administrators along with the dual language principals. After many years of implementation of dual language, the long-term success of their bilingual/biliterate graduates makes everyone proud that they all played a part in developing and maintaining this cutting-edge dual language program.

Teachers. We have heard teachers in dual language schools say things like, "This is heaven," or "I can't imagine teaching anywhere else." They also say, "I've never worked this hard in my life—but it's worth it." Visiting classrooms, we see the smiles on teachers' faces, the pride reflected in students' creativity, attitudes, and comments—"I can do anything in two languages—no problem!" Dual language teachers expect students to become profoundly proficient in the languages of instruction, grade by grade, through exploring in-depth academic themes that connect with the needs and reality of the community.

Teachers who are deeply proficient in the two languages of instruction are often also deeply bicultural. The cross-cultural experiences they have had in life lead to creativity in their teaching practices, as they create family and community in their classroom and want to share their intimate knowledge of varied cross-cultural ways of learning with their students. Monolingual English teachers who partner with the bilingual teachers also receive many of these benefits through the multicultural experiences that everyone in the program shares.

Planning time for teachers is an integral part of each school week in a dual language program. The shared resources and teaming that emerge from the planning process maximize the talents each teacher brings to the school. Heads together, teachers are often much more knowledgeable and insightful in curricular planning and responding to student behavioral concerns than when working alone. This can happen in team-teaching situations or within and across grade levels when dual language teachers are in self-contained classrooms. Dual language partners often support each other and become close colleagues, as well as friends. Because the curriculum is focused on multilingualism and multiculturalism and is accessible to everyone in the community, there is more encouragement for teachers to partner with parents in the learning process. Teachers make use of parents' knowledge and cross-cultural life experiences as resources for classroom learning.

Students. Proud, confident, excited, happy, collegial, caring … most students know they're attending the "awesome" program, and they show it in their hard work and their commitment to helping each other. It's not easy to be able to do math, science, social studies, art, music, and language arts through two languages, but students from severe poverty as well as other difficult circumstances have proven themselves capable of meeting the challenge. Whatever the contexts and characteristics of their lives, students from every corner of our community have thrived in dual language education, achieving at significantly higher levels than comparable groups schooled only through English. What is truly remarkable is that English learners in a dual language program can outpace native English speakers in monolingual English classes, making more progress each year on academic and linguistic development than native English speakers make.

Students speak proudly of their academic accomplishments, confident in their growing bilingualism and access to a greater world through their cross-cultural competency. Student graduates state that the program changed their lives. They find that as proficient bilinguals, they are highly desirable in the 21st century world of work, and they experience personal and professional richness that crosses cultures and languages.

Summary

So go for it! This model of schooling has more potential for changing the lives of students, teachers, administrators, and parents than almost any other school innovation. Dual language schooling is dramatically effective when implemented well. In fact, dual language is the most powerful school reform model for high academic achievement that we have seen in all our 28 years of conducting longitudinal studies in our field. Throughout this book, you will find all of our writing based on the research findings on dual language education to date, and with each topic, we will describe the range of implementation possibilities that we have seen. We dual language educators still have much more to learn, as every school program is a work in progress. But dual language education is now implemented in enough contexts throughout the U.S. that our collective experience can support success in every school community. Our time has come!

REFLECTIONS FROM THE FIELD

Bilingual educators throughout the United States have always had the burden of proof in demonstrating the benefits of learning a second language and at the same time, maintaining the richness of a maternal language that nourishes and defines the essence of our cultural identity in this global society. Throughout the years, anecdotal and local opinion were our only tools of defense and support in the holistic development of our students. The revolutionary work of Thomas and Collier unified and empowered educators and provided us with a common language. This empirical common language, complimented with processes and schemas provided by Thomas and Collier, has demonstrated without a doubt the effectiveness of bilingual education, regardless of the sociopolitical matrix that surrounds our field. At the national level, their longitudinal research and data has created an environment to develop additive instructional programs. In our district, this data has been instrumental not only in our move from transitional bilingual education into the dual language program models but also in the proliferation of a program in which two linguistic groups form part of one learning community where each and every student's language and culture are recognized.

WILMA VALERO

DIRECTOR, PROGRAMS FOR ENGLISH LANGUAGE LEARNERS
SCHOOL DISTRICT U-46
ELGIN, ILLINOIS

CHAPTER TWO: BEGINNINGS

The Evolution of Bilingual Schooling in the United States

Amazing! Or we might resort to Alice's words "curiouser and curiouser!" What a journey we bilingual educators have been through in the U.S., leading to what is now called dual language education. In essence, we have come full circle, as the original models of bilingual schooling that first developed in the 1960s have now become the preferred U.S. program for schooling all students through two languages. This historical overview provides important background for understanding how dual language schooling developed in the U.S., including some of the features that are considered essential to its success. In this chapter, we introduce program labels and terms used for dual language education and contrast these with other less effective programs designed only for English learners.

Two-way bilingual schooling in the U.S. As immigrants arrived in the United States from various regions of the world during the 1700s and 1800s, there was a period of openness to many languages. Public and private bilingual schools flourished during the 1800s in regions with large numbers of students of a non-English-speaking background (Kloss, 1998). Then, the U.S. went through a period of restricting the use of languages other than English during the late 1800s and continuing throughout the two world wars of the 1900s. But the booming postwar economy led to many societal changes, including the re-emergence of bilingual schooling.

Begun in 1963, the first two-way bilingual school researched, documented, and published was Coral Way Elementary School in Dade County, Florida (Mackey & Beebe, 1977). Cuban refugees who had settled in Miami after the 1959 revolution in their homeland brought with them qualified teachers who were academically proficient in Spanish. Given that the Cubans hoped to overthrow Castro and return to the island, they quickly established private bilingual schools that were in competition with the public schools. To avoid public school closure, the bilingual classes at Coral Way Elementary became a successful experiment to attract families to re-enroll their children in a Spanish/English program within the public school system.

At Coral Way Elementary, both native English and native Spanish speakers embraced the concept of acquiring the curriculum through the program's two languages. Instruction was provided half a day in each language (later known as one version of the 50:50 model). The Cuban students excelled, reaching grade-level curricular mastery in both English and Spanish. The native-English-speaking students also performed at and above grade level in English but did not quite reach grade level in Spanish, because this first experiment included more separation of the two groups than current models of two-way bilingual schooling. After this bilingual program demonstrated success in reaching grade-level achievement in English for both groups, even though these two-way students received only a half day of instruction in English, bilingual schooling soon spread to other public schools enrolling Mexican Americans in Texas, California, and New Mexico, and Navajo students in Arizona (Castellanos, 1983). By 1968, bilingual education was being provided in at least 56 locally initiated programs in 13 states. The large majority were Spanish-English programs, but six other languages were represented, including Navajo. In 1968-69, 76 bilingual programs in 70 different cities received the first U.S. federal funding for bilingual schooling. In addition to Spanish-English programs, funding went to bilingual schools teaching through English and Sioux, Pomo, Keresan, Navajo, Cherokee, Chinese, Cantonese, Japanese, Portuguese, or French (Andersson & Boyer, 1978).

Figure 2.1 illustrates the terms "two-way" and "one-way," used by linguists (Stern,1963) to describe demographic differences between varied program models for schooling through two languages. We have just discussed a two-way program at Coral Way Elementary School in Florida, and in the next section we turn to a one-way program in Canada. In Chapter 3, we will analyze in more depth the differences and similarities between two-way and one-way programs.

One-way bilingual schooling in Canada. In the same time frame, the first bilingual immersion school was established in St. Lambert, Canada in 1963 for English speakers to acquire the curriculum through French and English. This model of bilingualism for the "prestigious" group—those speaking the majority language—provided an interesting contrast to what was happening in the U.S. While this program was designed to reconcile socially separate language communities in Quebec (Spolsky & Cooper, 1977), it created the perhaps unanticipated consequence of producing Anglophone bilinguals who could successfully compete with French speakers in the French-speaking workplace, giving Anglophones increased social and economic mobility with wealth and dominance advantages (Baker, 2011).

In spite of this outcome, the program has spread throughout Canada and to this day remains dramatically successful, demonstrating that **students can study the curriculum using the non-majority language at least half of the instructional time with no loss to academic success in their primary language.** Evaluations of these programs continue to demonstrate students' high academic achievement, at or above grade level, when tested in both languages (Baker & Hornberger, 2001; Cummins & Swain, 1986; Genesee, 1987, 2007; Swain & Lapkin, 1982). While these English speakers develop very high levels of academic French, much higher than in foreign language classes, they are not completely comparable to native

Figure 2.1

Two-Way and One-Way
Dual Language Education

Two-Way	One-Way
Two language groups being schooled through their two languages; i.e., native English speakers attend dual language classes with native speakers of the partner language.	One language group being schooled through their two languages; i.e., students of one heritage language background attend dual language classes taught through English and the students' heritage language.
Two-way examples: (1) Native Spanish speakers and native English speakers work together in an integrated class, acquiring the grade-level school curriculum through Spanish and English. (2) Native Mandarin Chinese speakers and native English speakers work together in an integrated class, acquiring the grade-level school curriculum through Mandarin Chinese and English.	**One-way examples:** (1) Latino students entering in kindergarten may be fluent only in English, or proficient Spanish-English bilinguals, or fluent only in Spanish; but the heritage language of their ancestors is Spanish, or Spanish and English. These Latino students work together acquiring the grade-level school curriculum through Spanish and English. (2) Native English speakers acquire the curriculum through English and another language, as a foreign language/immersion program.

Copyright © 2012, W.P. Thomas & V.P. Collier. All rights reserved.

French speakers when tested with difficult grade-level tests in French. Since they are attending one-way, segregated programs only for English speakers, the students do not get the benefit of interactive dialogue with native-French-speaking peers in their classes, as would happen in a two-way model.

These Canadian bilingual programs use the term "immersion" in a unique way. They speak of "immersing" the native English speakers in the non-English language during the first two years of schooling. This has become what is known today as the 90:10 model—that is, 90% of the instructional time during kindergarten and first grade is in the minority, or less prestigious language, and only 10% of the instructional time in English. Immersion students who speak the prestigious, dominant language (English) learn to read in their second language before being introduced to reading in their first language. When English reading is formally introduced, the students have already developed an understanding of the concepts and conventions of reading, and they quickly reach grade level in English language arts. After the initial immersion experience, 90:10 models gradually increase instruction in English so that by fourth grade, fully half of the instructional time is spent in each respective language.

90:10 and 50:50 bilingual immersion in the U.S. As U.S. educators heard about the successful Canadian experiments, they began to implement different forms of this model in U.S. schools. In the 1970s and 1980s, 90:10 Spanish-English bilingual immersion became increasingly popular in a number of public schools throughout the state of California, as a two-way model, and in succeeding years spread to other states. Initially begun in a school in a subdivision of Los Angeles (Culver City) as a segregated one-way model for native English speakers, the teachers soon discovered that when they added native Spanish speakers to the classes, the English speakers' Spanish improved at a faster rate, and the program provided substantial benefits for the Spanish speakers (Cohen, 1976). The bilingual classes reduced negative stereotypes, led to increased friendships among the two language groups, raised the status of the Spanish language to a level equal to that of English, affirmed the students' bilingual/bicultural heritage, and led to increased academic achievement for both groups.

Foreign language educators in the U.S. also saw the benefits of bilingual immersion programs and began developing schoolwide models for native English speakers to receive their curricular subjects through another language as well as English. Some of these one-way schools for English speakers were 90:10, and others were 50:50 in cases where the parents were uncomfortable with the idea of 90% immersion in a non-English language during the early years of their children's schooling. However, evaluations of these one-way programs for English speakers found the 90:10 model to be the most successful in developing high academic proficiency in the second language (Collier, 1992; Genesee, 1987; Thomas, Collier & Abbott, 1993).

More recent longitudinal evaluations of two-way models have found that both language groups also experience the highest academic success in the 90:10 model, as compared to the 50:50 model (Collier & Thomas, 2009; Lindholm-Leary, 2001). At the same time, in the long term, both the 90:10 and the 50:50

models produce much higher academic achievement than monolingual schooling or transitional bilingual education.

Figure 2.2 illustrates the percentage of instructional time in each language in the 90:10 and 50:50 dual language program models, grade by grade. Another variation of the 90:10 program that is quite common is to start increasing the English instructional time to 20% in second grade rather than first grade, making it a 50:50 program by fifth grade. Chapter 3 will continue discussion of further important distinctions between these variations with the instructional time in each language.

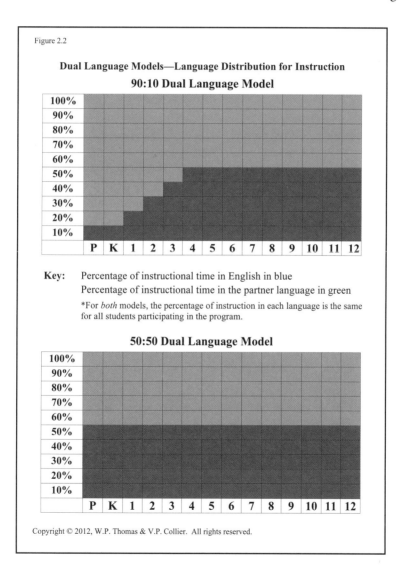

Figure 2.2

Dual Language Models—Language Distribution for Instruction

90:10 Dual Language Model

Key: Percentage of instructional time in English in blue
Percentage of instructional time in the partner language in green

*For *both* models, the percentage of instruction in each language is the same for all students participating in the program.

50:50 Dual Language Model

Copyright © 2012, W.P. Thomas & V.P. Collier. All rights reserved.

One of the essential components that still challenges many new implementers of two-way 90:10 dual language education is **the importance of providing the "90% immersion" experience for Grades PK-1 in the minority language, for both language groups.** The immersion experience means that the native English speakers learn to read first in the non-English language, while the speakers of the non-English language learn to read first in their native language. In other words, in this model both groups learn to read together in the non-English language, working together at all times. After two years with the majority of the instructional time (90%) spent in the non-English language, and only 10% of the instructional time in English, both groups are introduced to formal English reading in first or second grade. Teachers state that they do not need to re-teach reading, although there are conventions specific to each language that need to be explicitly taught. Both language groups already know how to read, and the process consists of applying strategies they are familiar with to the majority language, English.

The rationale for both groups initially receiving large amounts of curricular time in the minority language is that society provides a great deal of access to academic English outside of school, and much less for the minority language. **Thus both groups benefit from intensive initial "immersion" in the language less supported by the broader society.** This gives them a huge jump-start on acquisition of deep levels of academic proficiency in the non-English language, much of which transfers to English use, as English is gradually introduced into the curriculum. By keeping both groups together, the students support each other as language models and peer tutors when acquiring their second language. With peer language models present and the optimal components for natural first and second language acquisition in place, the magic of dual language immersion can begin. We will revisit this issue in more detail in the next chapters of this book.

The 90:10 program design that has developed in the U.S. for two-way, integrated bilingual immersion for all students is identical to the segregated Canadian one-way bilingual immersion model designed only for native-English speakers, with initial 90% immersion in the non-English language. However, those who oppose schooling in two languages and support the English-only movement have repeatedly misinformed the U.S. public by citing the Canadian immersion research as evidence that English learners should be "immersed" only in English. In fact, **"structured English immersion" is the exact opposite of the Canadian immersion model, and research shows that "immersion" in an all-English context leads to the lowest achievement levels for English learners** (Collier & Thomas, 2009, Figures 5.2 and 6.5). We caution you not to be fooled by this unprincipled mislabeling of the names of programs, just because both have the word "immersion" in the title. To illustrate some of the major differences between Canadian immersion and structured English immersion, see Figure 2.3.

Figure 2.3

Canadian Immersion	U.S. Structured English Immersion
Goal: Bilingualism/biliteracy	**Goal:** Monolingualism in English
Students: Native English speakers	**Students:** English learners
Teachers: Bilingual (French/English)	**Teachers:** Monolingual (English)
Classroom: Integrated—program is within school mainstream	**Classroom:** Segregated—only English learners enrolled
Additive: Students are developing both L1 and L2	**Subtractive:** Students are only developing L2 and losing L1
Minority language (French) has equal status with English.	**Minority languages** (native/heritage languages of students) are ignored.
Curriculum: Bilingual/bicultural	**Curriculum:** Monolingual

Copyright © 2012, W.P. Thomas & V.P. Collier. All rights reserved.

Transitional bilingual education. While all these initial experiments with integrated two-way bilingual schooling for Spanish and English speakers were maturing, several developments led to the expansion of segregated, one-way bilingual programs for non-English-speaking children. The first historical landmark was the federal Bilingual Education Act of 1968. The civil rights movement and the climate of social change of the 1960s led to the passage of several legislative bills with special funding for the education of minorities. The Bilingual Education Act focused on "children who come from environments where the dominant language is other than English." The three purposes of the 1968 act were to "(1) increase English-language skills, (2) maintain and perhaps increase mother-tongue skills, and (3) support the cultural heritage of the student" (Leibowitz, 1980, p. 24). A number of states followed the federal guidelines with their own legislation and funding for what generally became known as "transitional bilingual education." By 1971, 30 states had passed legislation either permitting or requiring some form of bilingual instruction for students of "limited English proficiency" (Ovando, Combs & Collier, 2006).

The name of this model emphasizes a transition to monolingual schooling in English as soon as bilingual/ESL teachers deem that each student is "ready." However, most transitional bilingual programs exit students after two to three years, before they reach grade-level achievement in English, typically with only half of their achievement gap closed. But at least the program provides a support system to assist students with development of literacy in their primary language and to keep up with grade-level schoolwork through their primary language while they work on acquiring English during a portion of each school day. This was an important first step for federal and state governments to take to expand opportunities for English learners. Primary language support is crucial for providing nonstop cognitive development, and developing literacy in primary language is key to literacy development in other languages.

However, two issues have lessened the success of this model. One is that English learners are segregated from their English-speaking peers while they are enrolled in transitional bilingual classes. In contrast, in two-way dual language programs, English speakers of the same age in the class serve as peer language models for natural English acquisition. The second issue is the short length of time spent in these bilingual classes with access to content and literacy development in their first language, typically two or three years. In Collier and Thomas (2009), we make the case that it takes an average of six years to reach grade-level academic achievement in the second language in a well-implemented program that uses the students' native language for instruction. Thus the typical transitional bilingual education program exits students, removing essential first language support, well before they have reached grade-level curricular mastery in English.

Ramírez (1992) coined the term "early-exit" transitional bilingual education and contrasted it with "late-exit" after he found that some schools had chosen to allow students to remain in transitional bilingual classes longer than two to three years. He found that English learners in late-exit programs that lasted five years or more were continuing to close the gap and reach grade-level achievement in English. English learners who were moved into all-English instruction after three years of bilingual support had closed half of the gap in English, but they remained at that relative level of achievement in each succeeding grade, continuing to make progress but no longer closing the gap once they joined mainstream English classes. In our longitudinal studies examining over 6 million student records in 35 school districts in 16 states (Collier & Thomas, 2009; Thomas & Collier, 1997, 2002), we found patterns similar to Ramírez's initial longitudinal studies. Significantly, only those students who attended two-way or one-way dual language programs for at least six to eight years completely closed the achievement gap in their second language.

Before continuing our chronological description of the evolution of dual language education, we pause to illustrate the programmatic contrasts between early-exit and late-exit transitional bilingual education and other subtractive models of schooling in which English learners gradually lose their first language as they acquire their second language, English. Figure 2.4 provides an overview of the main subtractive models of schooling for English learners that have developed in the U.S.

Figure 2.4

* Subtractive Models of K-5 Schooling for English Learners, from the most support to no support:

	Program Length	L1 Academic Support	Linguistic Emphasis	Cognitive Emphasis	Sociocultural Support
Transitional Bilingual Education — Late-exit	4-6 years	Moderate	Develops L1 and L2 Academic Proficiency	Moderate	Moderate, but segregated
Transitional Bilingual Education — Early-exit	2-3 years	Some	Partial L1 and L2 Academic Proficiency	Some	Some, but segregated
ESL Content/Sheltered Instruction	2-3 years	None	Academic English (only in L2)	Some	Some, but segregated
Structured English Immersion	1-2 years	None	Academic English (only in L2)	Little	Little, segregated
ESL Pullout	1-2 years	None	Only social English (only in L2)	Little	Little, segregated
Proposition 227 in California (as in law)	1 year	None	Only social English (only in L2)	None	Little or none, segregated
Submersion in English Mainstream	No program	None	No ESL support	No special cognitive support	None

- Subtractive bilingualism refers to students gradually losing their first language as the second language is acquired. This can lead to cognitive loss because of the crucial interconnection of first language with cognitive development.

Copyright © 2012, W.P. Thomas & V.P. Collier. All rights reserved.

over the past century, with late-exit transitional bilingual schooling providing the most support, Proposition 227 in California (one year of intensive ESL) the least support, and submersion in the English mainstream providing no special support at all. In the first book of this series (Collier & Thomas, 2009) we reviewed the research on these models and concluded that for English learners, only additive two-way and one-way dual language education have the potential to fully close the achievement gap with native English speakers.

As can be seen in Figure 2.4, late-exit transitional bilingual education comes the closest to providing the degree of support needed, but since it is a segregated model for English learners only, it often suffers from the social stigma of other isolated programs. Nevertheless, many of its characteristics are similar to that of a developmental or maintenance one-way bilingual program, to be described in the next paragraphs. Thus, this type of bilingual program has the potential to be transformed into a fully functioning dual language program.

Maintenance bilingual education. The term "maintenance" appeared in the late 1960s and became the most common name for one-way heritage language bilingual programs that had been established prior to the federal and state legislative initiatives. Maintenance programs taught through students' heritage language and through English contrast strongly with "transitional" or short-term programs. Maintenance programs provide content-area instruction in both languages equally for as many grades as the school system can provide the service. These programs are based on the UNESCO (1953) assertion that every child has the right to begin formal education in his/her mother tongue and to continue for as many years as the school system can provide. In the 1960s, the most typical maintenance models were designed for the elementary grades only. Ideally instruction through both languages would be provided for grades K-12, but secondary programs were rare at that time. These maintenance models were initially developed primarily in Spanish-speaking and indigenous communities of the Southwest U.S. Among the schools with high achievement were Navajo-English schools in Arizona (Rosier & Holm, 1980; Troike, 1978).

As transitional bilingual programs spread to all regions of the U.S. during the early 1970s, the "English-only" movement gained momentum by creating a dichotomy between transitional and maintenance programs (Epstein, 1977). Concerns were raised that native-language maintenance was not the task of the federal government, ignoring research evidence that maintaining grade-level achievement in first language led to higher achievement in second language. With each succeeding year, more of these maintenance programs lost their funding, even though the longitudinal research demonstrated that students reached higher levels of achievement in English when their native or heritage language was used for instruction for half of the instructional time. In spite of the fact that transitional bilingual education was designed only for newly arriving immigrants, these maintenance programs for heritage language speakers in the Southwest declined in numbers during the decade of the 1970s until the advent of dual language, which was initially named "developmental" (one-way) and "enrichment" (two-way).

Developmental, enrichment bilingual education. In 1984, with the federal reauthorization of the Bilingual Education Act, a new term was coined by James Lyons (1990), who authored the initial drafts of this new legislation. "Developmental" bilingual schooling emphasizes the natural, ongoing, developmental processes that children experience during the school years. **Thus was born the concept that social-emotional, cognitive, and linguistic processes are best developed in the two languages of the child across all curricular subjects, for as many years as possible.** The academic goals of this legislation were stated more precisely as allowing a child to meet grade-promotion and graduation requirements (Crawford, 1999), and thus to extend the program for more years and to close more of the achievement gap than shorter-term transitional bilingual education typically allowed. The term "developmental" was a breakthrough in moving away from the compensatory and remedial perspectives experienced in transitional programs to viewing bilingual education as an enrichment form of schooling. This 1984 reauthorization also extended the provisions of the 1978 law which stated that, where possible, developmental bilingual programs should enroll approximately equal numbers of native English speakers and English learners, but little federal funding was provided for this two-way model.

"Enrichment" is a term coined by Joshua Fishman (1976) to emphasize that bilingual schooling should also be made available to the linguistically dominant group in a society. Thus when developmental and enrichment concepts are combined, the program becomes two-way with two language groups studying the curriculum through two languages and expanding cross-cultural ways of thinking. This is an integrated model that enriches both majority and minority students' learning and leads to high academic achievement of all students.

The 1994 federal reauthorization moved even further away from remedial, compensatory models of bilingual schooling to an emphasis on enrichment and innovation. Two-way developmental bilingual programs were strongly encouraged, and some federal funding was for the first time provided for both language groups in a two-way program. This emergent federal support was again eliminated during the decade of the 2000s, and the English-only movement succeeded in passage of voter referenda in California, Arizona, and Massachusetts to limit the number of state-funded bilingual programs in those states. But these English-only efforts actually fueled the movement to implement more two-way dual language schools. One of the major turning points was the increasing advocacy of English-speaking parents who had experienced their own children's success in two-way schools and who therefore demanded that these programs remain in place for their children, as well as for the non-English-speaking families.

Dual language education. So we have journeyed full circle from the beginnings of bilingual schooling in the 20th century in the U.S., through decade after decade of influential political developments that eventually led to dual language education. The term "dual language education" has come from the politics of our field. When the various forms of bilingual education were attacked by proponents of the English-only movement, bilingual educators began to recognize that in the U.S. the term "bilingual education" had become negatively associated with schooling only for English learners. "Dual language" as a substitute for "bilingual" was being used among some bilingual educators to refer to bilingual schooling for all students (two-way programs). And the term has gradually become more popular as even some English-only advocates embraced two-way dual language for everyone.

Figure 2.5 summarizes the history that we have experienced in the U.S. and the pattern that appears to be evolving as each decade goes by. In this book we are combining all the names—enrichment, developmental, bilingual immersion, heritage language maintenance, and the variations of one-way and two-way, 90:10 and 50:50—under the umbrella term "dual language education." This book is focused on two-way and one-way models that welcome English learners and students of heritage language background into the same program and which also include native English speakers in two-way dual language classes.

Since a major focus of both our first book and this one is on English learners, we are not going to include reports on the research about one-way programs exclusively for

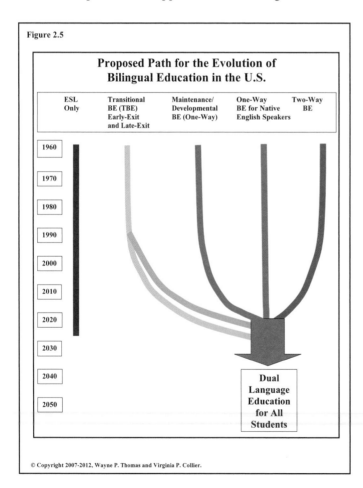

Figure 2.5

Proposed Path for the Evolution of Bilingual Education in the U.S.

| ESL Only | Transitional BE (TBE) Early-Exit and Late-Exit | Maintenance/ Developmental BE (One-Way) | One-Way BE for Native English Speakers | Two-Way BE |

1960
1970
1980
1990
2000
2010
2020
2030
2040
2050

Dual Language Education for All Students

© Copyright 2007-2012, Wayne P. Thomas and Virginia P. Collier.

native English speakers in this book. We are also choosing here not to focus on English as a Second Language (ESL) programs that provide no primary language support for students, nor are we focusing on transitional bilingual education. These remedial models were addressed in the first book in this series (Collier & Thomas, 2009). However, content ESL is a crucial component of every dual language program, so in this book we will address ESL within the context of schooling through two languages—English and the heritage language of the non-English speakers in the classroom.

As this chapter shows, dual language education started early in the 1960s and continued while the field developed and experimented with less effective strategies that responded to the politics of the times. For those of us who lived through these developments, it has been an adventure, to be sure!

Educadores bilingües a través de los Estados Unidos siempre se han confrontado con el reto de demostrar los beneficios del desarrollo de un segundo idioma a la vez que se mantiene la riqueza del idioma materno que nos nutre y forma la esencia de nuestra identidad cultural. A través de los años nuestras herramientas de defensa y apoyo para el desarrollo holístico de nuestros estudiantes en una sociedad global eran anecdóticas y de opinión local.

El trabajo de Thomas y Collier revolucionó nuestro campo uniéndonos y dándonos el poder de un trabajo colectivo que nos brinda un lenguaje en común. Este lenguaje empírico complementado con procesos y esquemas de Thomas y Collier demuestran, sin duda alguna, la efectividad de la educación bilingüe a pesar del matiz sociopolítico que rodea nuestro campo. La data presentada en sus estudios longitudinales creó el ambiente a nivel nacional para el desarrollo de programas instruccionales aditivos. En nuestro distrito esta data fue instrumental no sólo para hacer la transición al programa de lenguaje dual, pero también en la proliferación del programa donde ambos grupos lingüísticos forman parte de una sola comunidad educativa. Programas donde cada uno y cada cual reconocen en su idioma y su cultura elementos de intercambio educativo para el desarrollo del estudiante del hoy y del mañana en esta sociedad global.

WILMA VALERO,
DIRECTOR
PROGRAMS FOR ENGLISH LANGUAGE LEARNERS
SCHOOL DISTRICT U-46—ELGIN, ILLINOIS

Chapter Three:
Defining Dual Language Education

Reflections from the Field

The research and writings of Virginia Collier and Wayne Thomas have served as a starting point and ongoing guiding pillar for most dual language programs in Washington State. Their pertinent, targeted, long-term work has served as a solid foundation upon which is layered additional work by other researchers. When it comes to research on second language learners, the vast body of work by Collier and Thomas is regularly cited in our state and globally. They have been on a long mission of making dual language program information accessible to those striving to best meet the needs of dual language learners. Their work always paints a clearer picture of results achieved through high quality dual language education.

Michael Shapiro

Past President, Washington Association for Bilingual Education
Teacher, Madison Elementary Dual Language Enrichment Program
Mount Vernon, Washington

CHAPTER THREE:
DEFINING DUAL LANGUAGE EDUCATION

As seen in the last chapter, dual language schooling represents the best of all possibilities for uniting the needs of many diverse groups. In this second book, we are continuing to focus on the needs of English learners as our highest priority. But this school program is unique in bringing about a marriage of diverse interests into educational programs that meet common goals for everyone.

All of the names for enrichment dual language programs that evolved out of the history of bilingual schooling in the U.S. represent varieties of two-way and one-way dual language education. The umbrella term we are using in this book, dual language education, is the name that we see used most often in U.S. public school programs in recent years. An "old timer" in bilingual education recently said to us, "Why don't you just call it what it is—bilingual education!" But unfortunately the old term is associated with both remedial and enrichment models of bilingual schooling. So we're going with the new term that is quite popular in U.S. public schools, *dual language*, which best exemplifies the enrichment model of bilingual schooling, potentially for all students.

As seen in Figure 3.1, under the umbrella of dual language education in the U.S. we have a number of different historical names for additive, enrichment bilingual programs. We are classifying all of these as models that provide an additive bilingual context for all students; that is, the students receive nonstop support for both their first and second languages at least through puberty, which is the key to avoiding cognitive development slowdowns. In this context, all students can enjoy the tremendous cognitive advantages of additive bilingualism (Lambert, 1975, 1984). This is especially important for English learners, because it transforms their context for schooling into an experience with the same advantages that majority language students have.

The names under the umbrella include some historical names that have been used for dual language programs that we reviewed in the last chapter. Under both one-way and two-way, most programs are named the umbrella term, "dual language education," but because California's two-way programs historically grew out of the immersion models in Canada, their state's term is often "bilingual immersion." Some two-way programs have also used the term "dual immersion." In this book, we have chosen not to use the term "immersion" as an umbrella term, because that is historically associated with bilingual schooling only for native English speakers as developed in Canada. Additionally, the English-only movement has misused the term "immersion" as a subtractive model, as we illustrated in Figure 2.3 in the last chapter.

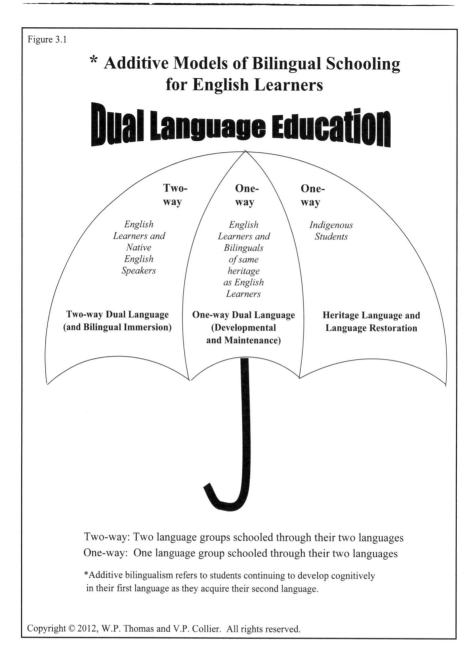

Figure 3.1

* Additive Models of Bilingual Schooling for English Learners

Dual Language Education

Two-way	One-way	One-way
English Learners and Native English Speakers	*English Learners and Bilinguals of same heritage as English Learners*	*Indigenous Students*
Two-way Dual Language (and Bilingual Immersion)	**One-way Dual Language (Developmental and Maintenance)**	**Heritage Language and Language Restoration**

Two-way: Two language groups schooled through their two languages
One-way: One language group schooled through their two languages

*Additive bilingualism refers to students continuing to develop cognitively
in their first language as they acquire their second language.

Copyright © 2012, W.P. Thomas and V.P. Collier. All rights reserved.

In this chapter and the next one, we will focus on the crucial characteristics of dual language education that make a huge difference for all students in the program. These definitions are so important to keep in mind as a program is being developed and refined that we ask you to ponder each of these points carefully so that you have a clear understanding of the reasons that staff developers guide educators to take seriously each step in the design of the program. In this book, our definitions are research derived and research driven. Our reporting here is from real-life school contexts in our research findings from dual language schools. We take the position that research findings can clearly guide practice and should inform school decisions made about dual language program design and implementation. One of these dual language decisions for which our research findings have provided some guidance is the distinction between one-way and two-way programs, to be discussed in the next section.

Demographics: One-way and two-way

Many authors and researchers in our field often overlook important demographic factors in dual language education. Because of this, we consider it important to acknowledge one-way as well as two-way demographic contexts, because we have analyzed large databases of longitudinal student achievement data, and our research findings have strong, positive implications for all of these varying demographic mixes in dual language programs. Over the years the term "dual language" has been defined by some researchers as applying only to two-way programs with equal numbers of native English speakers and students from the other language background while ignoring one-way. We take the position that **one-way is equally as effective as two-way in the long term and that both are enrichment models of dual language education**.

One-way. The distinction between one-way and two-way originated with Stern (1963). One-way refers to one language group receiving their schooling through their heritage language and another language. This group can be the privileged speakers of the majority or dominant language, or it can be the speakers of a minority language (including those whose grandparents spoke the language, but who currently may no longer speak it or possess only a receptive fluency). However, in this book we have chosen not to review research on one-way programs exclusively for native English speakers, since those are foreign language programs that do not focus on serving the needs of culturally and linguistically diverse students.

Therefore, when we refer to one-way dual language programs in this book, we are speaking of programs in which minority language speakers are enrolled and the full curriculum is taught through English and the minority language (i.e., Spanish, Mandarin, Arabic), which we will refer to as the *heritage language*, or the *partner language* of a dual language program. For example, in Dearborn, Michigan, there are excellent Arabic-English programs for speakers of the Arabic language. These may be classified as two-way if they have some native English speakers attending the classes. When most or all of the students are of Arabic-speaking heritage, the dual language school is a one-way program, even when some of these students speak only English when they first enter the program.

Along the border with French-speaking Canada, there are francophone contexts in which almost all of the students are of French-American heritage. While these students may speak mainly English, their parents' recent past was mostly French-speaking and they are living in a French heritage language context, a natural opportunity for developing one-way French-English dual language schools. In Texas, New Mexico, Arizona, and California, there are many schools near the border with Mexico that have very few native English speakers. These are mostly one-way Spanish-English contexts for instruction.

Individual schools throughout the southwest U.S. may also be one-way contexts in demographic areas where Spanish speakers are isolated from English speakers. This sometimes occurs in rural communities, and it can also be a common demographic context in urban areas where neighborhoods tend to be defined by ethnic groups, often accentuated by socioeconomic circumstances. Urban demographic patterns throughout the U.S. often have developed neighborhoods of isolated ethnic groups, resulting in neighborhood schools dominated by students of one heritage language background. At the same time, throughout the U.S. there are many urban schools with a great mixture of languages represented in the student population; for example, there are as many as 70 different languages among the ESL students of one regional subdivision of schools in Chicago.

Another important context for the development of one-way dual language programs is within indigenous communities such as the well established Navajo and Zuni bilingual programs in Arizona and New Mexico, Hawaiian in Hawaii, Cherokee in North Carolina, and Yup'ik in Alaska (Francis & Reyhner, 2002). "From an indigenous perspective, the mother language serves as a basic and fundamental source of identity, sacredness, and strength of an individual, family, and community" (Romero, 2007, p. 493). In New Mexico, each of the 19 pueblos has its own unique heritage language, some of which are not written languages. As each of the pueblos embraces the significance of language restoration, their one-way dual language programs in the schools within their communities are governed by their tribal leaders, honoring the uniqueness of each language, and leading to significantly improved student attendance and achievement in English (C. Sims, personal communication, November 12, 2011).

Two-way. In the U.S., to classify a school or classroom as two-way, we have found that at least 1/3 of the students in the dual language program should be native English speakers and/or native/heritage speakers of the partner language. Because this is an integrated model, the ideal conditions for natural, subconscious acquisition of the second language are then present. Native speaking peers for both languages provide opportunities for interactive exchange (i.e., modeling) among students as they explore and problem-solve across the curricular activities. Other researchers often speak of an ideal two-way context as one where 50% of the students are native English speakers and the other 50% are speakers of the partner language. But, the reality of our community school demographics sometimes limits our ability to reach that 50:50 balance of languages. Research ideals and practical realities can bring dual language educators to a compromise that works. When the percentage of native English speakers goes below 35%, dual language may still work, but the context for instruction becomes more of a one-way program. In fact, we have found in our research that **dual language education is the most powerful school reform for high academic achievement, whatever the demographic mix.** The only difference between two-way and one-way is the presence of native English speakers in the two-way classroom. Dual language is the same enrichment program, whether two language groups are involved or just one.

Does two-way or one-way make a difference? Does it matter what type of demographic context your school has? Our ongoing research tells us "No!" We have found that students in one-way dual language programs with high quality instruction and well-defined program implementation can achieve at equally high levels in the second language (English) to their counterparts attending a two-way dual language program and far better than their peers in a non-dual language program. However, students in two-way contexts generally reach grade-level achievement in English one or two years earlier than students in one-way contexts. And yet in the long term, both groups are able to reach grade level and beyond in their second language (see Figure 6.1).

This is an important message, because often parents and community members are convinced that their English learners should only attend the English mainstream, thinking that it will help their children learn English as fast as possible. As we showed clearly in our first book in this series (Collier & Thomas, 2009), choosing all-English instruction in the mainstream is the worst choice the community can make for the English learner. Mainstream English instruction for English learners leads to the lowest achievement over time, with many of these students dropping out before completing high school. Those who stay are among the lowest achievers in school, at the 9th-12th percentile (22nd-25th NCE) (Collier & Thomas, 2009, pp. 77-79). We and other researchers call this *submersion*, an English-only mainstream classroom with no alternative language supports, in contrast with enriched bilingual immersion through two languages (i.e., dual language education). (See Figure 4.9 in the next chapter for an illustration of this data.)

The reason that we are emphasizing that students attending one-way programs are equally capable of reaching grade-level achievement in the second language is that some researchers have taken the stance that two-way is the only way to implement dual language. Two-way dual language education may be ideal, but if your demographics do not include sufficient numbers of native English speakers, you can still have a dual language program. Our research is clear that dual language can flourish in all demographic contexts, both one-way and two-way. Therefore, schools should not use their demographics as an excuse to avoid teaching through two languages. When there are a sufficient number of students of one heritage language background, when the families understand fully the benefit of enrichment schooling through their two languages, and when there are committed, certified bilingual teachers available to teach curricular subjects through the heritage language, it is a win-win for everyone—students, teachers, families, the school district, and the local and global community.

For example, Woodburn, Oregon, has had a group of Russian-heritage speakers who immigrated to Oregon in the 1960s and requested a dual language program for their children. This Russian-English program continues to flourish and has led to the establishment of Spanish-English dual language classes for the remainder of the students, 78% of whom are of Spanish-speaking background. Some classes are one-way and others two-way, with the school district committed to dual language for all students and all grades K-12.

In the planning process, bilingual staff will need to be clear about the demographic mix of each dual language class and plan accordingly for the language and curricular needs of each individual student, but within the context of integrated activities for all. Each bilingual teacher can create an ongoing profile of each student's linguistic and cultural background, language proficiency levels attained in the two languages of instruction, and growth in each curricular area. Dual language teachers almost always teach in challenging cross-cultural mixes with students at varied proficiency levels in the two languages. The joy is to create a sense of community in the classroom, whatever the demographic mix.

Language Distribution: 90:10 or 50:50

Another dual language program decision to address in the early stages of planning is the amount of instructional time to be spent in each language. All elementary school programs eventually have a 50:50 time allocation by the mid- to upper-elementary grades, with the instructional time for one year divided equally between the two languages. The ratios 90:10, 80:20, 70:30, 60:40, and 50:50 are potential choices for the initial grades of the program, but 90:10 (sometimes 80:20) and 50:50 are the most common choices for the early elementary grades (see Figure 2.2). We will illustrate by discussing the main contrasts between 90:10 and 50:50.

90:10. The 90:10 program may seem difficult to explain and sell to parents at first, but this model has demonstrated success in Canada since the early 1960s and in the U.S. since the 1970s, with high student achievement outcomes for students participating in the 90:10 dual language classroom (Baker, 2011; Collier & Thomas, 2009; Genesee, 1987; Lindholm-Leary, 2001). As illustrated in Chapter 2 (see Figure 2.2), the 90:10 model begins by "immersing" the students 90% of the time in the minority language (also "partner language" in this book) for the first two years of schooling (preschool and kindergarten, or kindergarten and first grade). Classroom experiences in the English 10% of the time must be focused on ESL/ELD and include structured oral language activities that extend what the students are doing in the partner language. These planned, intentional activities might include aspects of art, music, and/or physical education, but these specials alone are not enough to support academic language development in English and should be taught by a licensed ESL teacher.

In the first one to three years of the program, literacy is developed in the partner language (not English) for all, including native English speakers, in a two-way program. One example of how the program progresses toward 50% of instruction in English is as follows: in kindergarten, 90% of the instruction is in Spanish; in first grade the ratio may change to 80:20 and early literacy experiences in English are added; second grade is 70:30; third grade is 60:40; and by fourth grade equal instructional time is provided in both languages. In the 90:10 model, the general concept being implemented is intensive work in the early school years in the non-English or partner language to develop a comfort level with oral fluency, a literacy base, and substantial vocabulary. Then after one, two, or three years of a strong foundation built in the partner language, formal literacy instruction in English is added. Gradually increasing instructional time in English helps students transfer skills from the partner language and make structured progress in acquiring oral and literacy skills in English across the curriculum.

50:50. The 50:50 model of language distribution emphasizes, from the first year of schooling, an equal percentage of instructional time through English and the partner language. This seems simpler to implement than 90:10, but teachers of 90:10 classes advocate that it is clearer to the students to learn to read in the partner language first (sequential biliteracy). Then after one or two years of literacy development in the partner language, when reading/writing in English is explicitly introduced, the students quickly make accelerated progress in written English acquisition, because they have already learned to read and write in the other language (Genesee, Paradis & Crago, 2004).

Therefore, one major contrast between 90:10 and 50:50 is *sequential versus simultaneous biliteracy acquisition*. Most 50:50 dual language programs teach students to read and write in both languages from kindergarten on (simultaneous biliteracy), while 90:10 dual language programs emphasize sequential biliteracy development. In 50:50 programs, explicit teaching of listening, speaking, reading, and writing skills takes place within thematic language arts instructional blocks for each language. For the remainder of the curricular subjects taught through thematic units connected to the language arts blocks, half of the material is taught in English and the other half in the partner language. Math, science, and social studies, as well as the specials, are best interwoven into themes that are an integral part of the explicit language arts objectives.

What does the research on simultaneous versus sequential biliteracy tell us? The jury is still deliberating. Some studies show that one is better than the other, but overall, in the long term both seem to work reasonably well; however, few studies have addressed this issue explicitly (Lindholm-Leary, 2009). Canadian researchers have generally concluded that sequential biliteracy in the 90:10 model works best in one-way programs for native English speakers, at least in the short term (Cummins & Swain, 1986). Again, we remind dual language educators that when implementing sequential literacy within either a one-way or two-way 90:10 program, in kindergarten, native English speakers are initially taught to read in their *second* language , followed by formal English reading/writing instruction added to the curriculum by second grade. In a two-way 90:10 program, the English learners are taught to read in their *first* language, followed by formal English reading/writing instruction added by second or third grade.

Many dual language schools base their decisions regarding 90:10 or 50:50 on the research findings that 90:10 is more effective (Collier & Thomas, 2009; Lindholm-Leary, 2001). This research shows that in the early grades, both language groups benefit from deeper proficiency development in the partner language (less supported by the broader society), which influences students' success in the upper elementary grades in both languages. Furthermore, 90:10 students completely close the achievement gap in English sooner than 50:50 students. At the same time, decision makers can also be influenced by attitudes regarding the model that the community is prepared to support. The main concerns are often students' and parents' comfort levels and teachers' confidence that the 90:10 program will work well for their students. The availability of qualified bilingual teachers can also be an issue, since fewer monolingual English-speaking staff are needed in the first two years of a 90:10 model (Soltero, 2004).

Moreover, a significant percentage of dual language schools that start as a 50:50 model choose to shift to a 90:10 model after several years of implementation, with 90% of instruction in the partner language for all students at least in pre-school and kindergarten. This is because the teachers receiving these dual language students in the upper grades become concerned that both language groups need deeper academic proficiency in the partner language to do challenging grade-level work in that language, especially as the cognitive difficulty is increased grade by grade. **The 90:10 model provides a stronger foundation in the language less supported by the broader society, for both language groups, at no cost to their English success in the long term** (Cloud, Genesee & Hamayan, 2000; Collier & Thomas, 2009; Escamilla, 2000; Genesee, 1987; Goldenberg, 2000; Howard, Christian & Genesee, 2003; Lindholm-Leary, 2001; Lindholm-Leary & Borsato, 2006; Ramírez, 1992; Willig, 1985).

In a 50:50 two-way program, both language groups, taught together, benefit from formal language arts instruction provided for each language. The teacher guides students as they work together in intentionally structured activities, providing language support to each other during their language arts and content instruction time. Therefore, **we recommend that the groups not be separated for initial reading instruction in their native language, because this lowers test scores both in English and in the partner language in the long term.** (This is a practice that is common in Texas, but less common in other states.) In a two-way class, when the two language groups are separated for language arts time and each taught reading in their native language first, there is a discrepancy in the number of overall minutes for instruction in English and the partner language. For native English speakers, this adds significant instructional minutes in English, resulting in substantially less than 50% of the total instructional minutes in the partner language. This compromises the non-negotiable dual language component that requires a minimum of 50% of instruction to be delivered through the partner language (see Figure 3.2). In this case the English speakers may not receive adequate instructional time in the partner language, leading to difficulties as the curriculum becomes more complex and cognitively demanding over time. Both groups also lose precious instructional interaction with each other at this young age, when peer language modeling and teaching is a key factor in second language acquisition. In this 50:50 model, if both language groups are allowed to stay together for both the English language arts time as well as the partner language arts time, then 50% instructional time is truly honored in each language, and the two groups support each other, serving as peer teachers for both languages, and their long-term test scores are higher (Collier & Thomas, 2009)**.**

If 90:10 sequential biliteracy is your program choice, both language groups will especially flourish as they work together, first in the partner language, followed by increasing instructional time in English. As stated before, the research findings from around the world clearly indicate that speakers of the minority/partner language who are just beginning acquisition of English do best when their primary language is used in their initial literacy development (Baker, 2011; Cummins, 2000b; Dutcher, 2001; Skutnabb-Kangas, Phillipson, Mohanty & Panda, 2009). Native English speakers, on the other hand, have succeeded quite well when they learn to read first in their second language (the partner language). Why? For several reasons, including that English is the language of power—and the world and our students know that. They know that English, the dominant language, is not going to be taken away from them and that their identity is secure. Furthermore, many English speakers have already begun to read in English before starting school, with access to environmental print, television, and the Internet in English, their first language. English speakers are surrounded by uses of English outside of school (Freeman, Freeman & Mercuri, 2005). Thus it is not necessary to have English speakers learn to read in English first before being formally introduced to reading in the partner language. Both language groups can work together, either acquiring the two languages' written systems in the same year, or in sequential years.

Measuring time in each language

Once the decision has been made as to what percentage of instructional time will be provided in each language for each grade level, the next step is to examine the minutes experienced per language, to see that the appropriate balance is provided. The first non-negotiable for dual language classes is that at least 50% of the instructional time must be in the partner language with NO MORE than 50% in English.

Figure 3.2

Non-Negotiable Components of Dual Language Education

- At least 50% of the instructional time must be taught in the non-English (partner) language

- Separation of the two languages for instruction

- PK/K-12 commitment

Copyright © 2009, D. Rogers. All rights reserved.

Why? … For the same reasons as stated above. The dominant language is the power language, the one that gets all the emphasis, all the attention, and all the status in the broader society, while Spanish and other minority languages are often vilified in current political rhetoric in the U.S. (Gándara & Hopkins, 2010). Students have greater access to English outside of school as well as inside school. The challenge is to get across the message that the partner language is equally valued, and that students who speak the partner language are respected as equal peers/colleagues in the learning process. Also, a major goal of the program is full proficiency in both of the languages. This is not easy because even for a partner language such as Spanish, curricular materials and authentic literature are not as easily available and accessible as materials in English, especially in the upper grades. Finding bilingual teachers who are both certified in the subject areas to be taught and academically proficient in the language of instruction is another significant challenge for schools and districts committed to providing K-12 dual language. In addition, these teachers need to be knowledgable about the underlying principles and practices of second language acquisition methodology with dual language education.

But teachers take on the challenge, and year by year as dual language programs mature, schools commit to purchase, develop, and collect better quality materials that fully support exciting bilingual/bicultural teaching. So count the instructional minutes, and that includes language arts, math, science, social studies, music, art, physical education, library, computer lab, science lab, reading groups, special needs classes, one-on-one tutoring support, field trips, assemblies …. Every minute in school counts. Even when no formal teaching is taking place, natural language acquisition is occurring. We acquire language by using that language in natural and interesting and meaningful contexts. Is more of the total school time at your school conducted in English than in the partner language? Then the school community must sit down together and re-design the schedule, as well as reconsider the use of the partner language in the larger school community, until the appropriate balance between the two languages is achieved.

Separating the two languages for instruction

Here we address another program decision, which is the second non-negotiable for dual language programs. For the early grades, it is important to separate the two languages by teacher, or time, or subject. Most researchers of bilingual schooling strongly recommend that in order to build deep academic proficiency in both languages of instruction, separation of the two languages should be formally addressed in the program design at the planning stage (see Figure 3.3).

Some of the rationale for this language separation comes from the research on transitional bilingual classes, in which bilingual teachers in self-contained

Figure 3.3

Separation of the Two Languages

By teacher	**Team teaching:** • One teaches in English in one classroom; the other teaches in the partner language in the other classroom located next door or across the hall.
By time in each language	**E.g., 50:50 model:** • Alternate mornings and afternoons • Alternate by one day **Only after students are more proficient in their L2:** • Alternate every two days, or • Alternate every other week
By subject	The first year, some subjects are taught in one language and the rest in the other language, with language arts taught in both languages. In subsequent years, the subjects alternate to the other language, so students wrestle cognitively and acquire vocabulary/language discourse in both languages for all subjects. Thematic units provide scaffolding and natural learning connections between the two languages, with different material covered in each language.

Copyright © 2012, W.P. Thomas & V.P. Collier. All rights reserved.

classes often switched back and forth between the two languages of instruction, to reinforce concepts, to translate for the recently arrived immigrants, to illustrate comparisons between the two languages, and to naturally use code-switching, which is common in bilingual communities. Sometimes this language switch was due to the teacher being more proficient in one language and less proficient in the other one. This common language switching strategy among transitional bilingual teachers led to mixed results in language development for students, with some students not reaching their full potential in one or both of the languages of instruction. Within a language-switching scenario, students building skills in their second language could tune out or daydream while one language was being used, because they knew the material would be repeated in the other language (Legarreta, 1979, 1981; Milk, 1986). The students thus received less productive instructional time in general, leading to lower academic achievement, as well as less development of the students' weaker language. By clearly separating the two languages through the program design and providing high quality sheltered instruction in both languages, both of these potential problems can be avoided.

By teacher. If several teachers are more academically proficient in one language and less in the other, a team-teaching model may be the most appropriate for the program, pairing each monolingual English-speaking teacher (ESL- or TESOL-trained) with a bilingual teacher who will teach in the partner language. This can vary from grade to grade, depending upon the staff available for the program, and their proficiency levels in the two instructional languages. Some of the upper grade classes may be self-contained when the teacher is deeply proficient in both languages of instruction. Alternatively, schools may decide that there is power and encouragement for second language use when one teacher instructs in only one language. Team-teaching is also a way to use valued monolingual English staff who are invested in the program and eager to partner with a bilingual teacher. In fact, programs that use this teacher-pairing strategy frequently report fewer personnel changes and greater instructional effectiveness overall. We recommend this strategy as a pragmatic way of best utilizing the talents of participating teachers and increasing the cognitive level of instruction in both languages.

Typically when team teaching is utilized, each teacher in a team has his/her own classroom, with the two classrooms located next to each other or across the hall. Using Korean as an example for the partner language, one classroom can be designated as the Korean world and the other classroom as the English world. This allows the teacher of each classroom "world" to surround the students with linguistic and cultural experiences appropriate to each language, and defines a clear separation between the two languages. To be cost-effective, the two teachers who are exchanging classes are assigned two classes of students that alternate between the two rooms. In this situation, the hard-to-find qualified bilingual teacher can serve twice as many dual language students by providing instruction in the partner language.

By time. Many dual language programs choose to separate the two languages by time in the schedule. Using the 50:50 model as an example, some programs divide the instructional day, with morning in one language and afternoon in the other language. If this half-day plan is chosen, it is very important to switch which language is taught in the morning by the second semester or at the end of each quarter-year, since morning time is the more efficient learning time. This keeps the equitable balance in development of the two languages. **While students are in the initial**

stages of building proficiency in their second language, it is important that they receive instructional time in both languages fairly often, making natural connections between L2 and L1, so this half-day choice is an appropriate decision, especially for the beginning grades in the program.

A second choice is to separate the languages by a whole day—English is the language of the day today and tomorrow the partner language is the language of the day. In communities that are natural bilingual contexts in which students have access to both languages outside of school time, separation by day seems to work reasonably well for the beginning grades. A third choice for the upper grades, when students are more proficient in the two languages, is to separate by alternating the language of instruction every two days. Within a four-week period, both languages will have experienced equal instructional time (since Mondays and Fridays can vary in intensity). Another two-day pattern of some programs is to do Monday and Tuesday in one language, Wednesday and Thursday in the other language, and on Friday, half a day in each language. Some schools in the upper grades, after students have acquired deep proficiency in both languages, separate the languages by a whole week, or occasionally by thematic units. But **we do not recommend the two-day or whole-week alternation in the early grades because beginning students need more frequent exposure to both languages in the early years of second language acquisition.**

By subject. A third very common strategy is to separate the two languages by subject. For example, this year math and English language arts and specials could be taught in English, while science and social studies are taught in the partner language, along with language arts in the partner language. To acquire the academic vocabulary for each subject in both languages, next year social studies and science can be in English, along with English language arts, while math and partner language arts and specials are taught in the other language. There are some dual language models that choose to stay with one instructional language for one subject throughout the early grades, but **from research findings to date on this issue, we recommend giving students opportunities to develop academic language for all subjects, by alternating which language is used for each subject throughout the course of the program.**

Reasons not to rigidly separate the two languages. Now that for program planning purposes we have made a strong case for programmatic separation of the two languages for teachers' delivery of instruction, we are also presenting some exceptions to this "rule" when it comes to L2 production by the student, as seen in Figure 3.4. For example, although clear expectations will be set for language use in L1 and L2, children just beginning to acquire the second language

Figure 3.4

Reasons Not to Rigidly Separate
the Two Languages

Clear expectations should be set for language use in L1 and L2,
BUT there are reasons not to rigidly separate the two languages:

- For beginning second language acquisition, each teacher should strictly separate the two languages.

- Young children (PK-K-1) may respond in their language of comfort. But after 2-3 years of second language development, children can be expected to use only the language of instruction.

- As students build skills in the two languages, they must be able to explore cross-lingual, metalinguistic patterns, at all grade levels, such as:
  - o Cognates
  - o Reading skills across the two languages
  - o Grammatical similarities and differences
  - o Nonverbal patterns across different contextual uses
  - o Patterns in code-switching
  - o Writing style variations in different genres
  - o Standard varieties and regional dialects
  - o At high school level, using bilingualism in service to the community, including skills of translation

Why?

- To strengthen metacognitive "muscle"
- To raise metalinguistic awareness
- To explicitly support students' transfer of skills and strategies from one language to the other

Copyright ©2012, W.P. Thomas & V.P. Collier. All rights reserved.

should be allowed to respond/speak in whatever language(s) they feel most comfortable, safe, and secure. So language separation in the early stages of second language acquisition is expected of the teacher, but moves from "encouraged" to "required" for the students as they progress through the earlier years (2-3) of the program.

Young children in PK-1 may respond in their language of choice in the earlier years; however, schools and classrooms should have a clear expectation for language use (especially L2 use) that starts the first day of school. Children are expected to use some L2 in the first year of the program, but as they begin to develop oral academic proficiency in their L2, they should be encouraged and required to use that language in social and academic settings. At that stage of second language development, it is appropriate for students to develop their ability to communicate and to sustain academic conversations without switching to the other language. This pushes the students to acquire a deeper and deeper range of language functions, structures, and vocabulary in each language across all content areas. The teacher, therefore, must provide both the support and the expectation for students' use of their second language.

As students move to deeper proficiency in each language, in the upper grades there are also instructional reasons to explore the two languages together in natural contexts (Cummins, 2008; de Jong, 2011). While this may be especially important in upper elementary and secondary classrooms, **it is important for this metalinguistic awareness to be intentionally developed at all grade levels.** As students become increasingly expert with linguistic patterns of their two languages, lessons should explore cognates, grammatical similarities and differences, nonverbal patterns across varied contextual uses of the two languages, writing style variations in different writing genres, the unconscious rules that govern code-switching patterns among bilinguals in the school community, standard varieties of the two languages compared with regional dialects and their sociolinguistic usage, and on and on. In addition, when bilingual students reach high school level, they are going to be called on to explore many professional contexts where they will be using their bilingualism in service to the community, and knowing how to translate and understanding the responsibilities of translators are life skills that bilingual adults are expected to master (Sizemore, 2011).

The duration of the dual language program

There is one more crucial planning decision for dual language education: for how many grades will the program continue? The research has clearly shown that in two-way dual language contexts, it takes an average of six years to reach grade-level curricular mastery in second language (Collier & Thomas, 2009; Cummins, 1981; Lindholm-Leary, 2001). Therefore, it is a non-negotiable that dual language programs must continue for at least six years, K-5 or PK-5. But that is just a minimum, and in one-way contexts with few native English speaking peers, English learners may need up to eight years to reach grade-level achievement in second language. That means that the dual language program should continue through the middle school years, K-8 or PK-8. **We highly recommend that each**

**school district implementing dual language education plan for a continu-
ation throughout all the school years, to fully realize the potential of K-12
dual language education. That is the ideal.** Many programs have developed
K-8, and some PK-8, but fewer have extended the program all the way through
the high school years. Ysleta Independent School District in El Paso, Texas was
one of the earliest pioneers to create a complete PK-12 dual language program.
More than ten years later, their program graduates find a range of post-secondary
and career opportunities available to them, attesting to the transformative power
of rigorous, student-centered, leadership-oriented dual language education. Now
more districts are following in their footsteps.

Growing the program grade by grade. Most two-way dual language programs start in an elementary school with kindergarten classes the first year (or
if a preschool already exists the program might start with PK-K) and grow the
program grade by grade, adding a new grade level each year. That gives the
English speakers the experience of acquiring the partner language in the early
grades when the curriculum should provide a natural discovery-learning context
for language acquisition through child-centered instructional practice. Typically,
no new native English speakers are admitted to the program after first grade un-
less they already have fluency in the partner language, because the curriculum is
cognitively more demanding with each succeeding grade, and proficiency in the
language is needed to keep up with grade-level work. On the other hand, newly
arriving English learners can benefit so dramatically from the program that they
may be admitted at any grade level, as long as parallel ESL support is provided
for them. In particular, the new arrivals who have received formal schooling in
their home country can be a great resource as language models and peer teachers
during the partner language instructional time, and they can stay on grade level
in their mother tongue (partner language) while working on acquiring English.

Implementing several grades in one year. One-way dual language programs
also typically start in an elementary school with kindergarten or PK-K classes, and
grow the program grade by grade. But if the bilingual teacher resources are already
available, the students have grown up in a bilingual community in which they are
orally proficient in the two languages, and the community is eager to jump-start
the program, it is possible to accelerate the number of grades implementing dual
language classes in the one-way context. Implementation of dual language schooling in several grades in one year (e.g., K-2) can present quite a challenge in finding
both curricular materials and bilingual teacher resources, but it does happen in
bilingual communities that are willing and able to take on the challenge.

Summary

Given the length of time that it takes to reach grade-level achievement in second language—an average of six to eight years—it is important that parents who enroll their children in dual language programs take time to study and fully understand the commitment needed for students to be successful in the program over time. To assist all students, including new arrivals at all grade levels, the school community should advocate for K-12 dual language programs. Parents who see the tremendous advantages of this enrichment program for all students are also responsible for advocacy with other families of the school community. These dual language programs evolve into an innovation that influences the whole community as families help to prepare their students to become contributing multilingual and multicultural community members and true global citizens of the 21st century.

Reflections from the Field

"The dual language program changed the life I was going to have in many ways. With time I became better in English and in Spanish. In high school I chose to take classes in both languages and graduated with the Bilingual Seal... When I attended college, I decided to pursue two majors, one in Political Science, for my love of politics, and one in Spanish, for my love of my native language and culture... "

Cynthia Jiménez

Cynthia Jiménez, pictured above with classmates Luis Carlos Muñoz and Octavio Muñoz, shares her own ELL experiences with state-wide educational leaders. In third grade, Cynthia was forced out of a bilingual classroom and into structured English immersion under Proposition 227 in California. Soon after, her family moved to New Mexico, and Cynthia enrolled in a dual language middle school. Although initially reluctant, Cynthia and her family now attribute much of her success (and that of her siblings) to her participation in dual language. Cynthia is currently double-majoring in Political Science and Spanish at the University of New Mexico, and she says, "I will graduate soon and I know I will use my expertise and advantage in both languages to help other students who are like me."

Edward Tabet-Cubero

Deputy Director

Dual Language Education of New Mexico

CHAPTER FOUR: UNIQUE QUALITIES OF DUAL LANGUAGE EDUCATION

Once you have defined differences in demographic characteristics (one-way and two-way), variations in language distribution (90:10, 80:20, 50:50), and the three major non-negotiables of dual language education (K-12 commitment, separation of the two languages, at least 50% of the curriculum taught in the partner language), additional implementation decisions remain. These decisions include students to be served, recruitment of teachers and staff, instructional practices and staff development, and community advocacy.

Students

Who will the dual language program serve? From the previous chapter, you know that we encourage educators to find ways to provide dual language classes for all students. Given any demographic context, all students in your school district will benefit from these classes. Often parents may initiate the process of envisioning the program, or perhaps a determined principal who has seen dual language at work in other schools will start the momentum that leads to program implementation. At the central administrative level, initiatives may begin with a visionary superintendent, as well as one or both of the coordinators of bilingual/ESL and foreign language education. Initial program start-up is based upon interested principals, available bilingual teacher resources, and support of the school community.

English learners. But the first and most important decision should be based on the students who need the most support, and that group is the English learners. When English learners enter your school district at the beginning level of proficiency in the English language, initially they are the students typically placed at greatest risk. Their initial assessment in English defines the most significant achievement gap with the native English speaking students of all at-risk groups (see Collier & Thomas, 2009, for a full explanation). The most effective route to their eventual high academic achievement in English is dual language education. Through participation in the dual language program, English learners can stay on grade level in their native language and acquire the full curriculum in the language they know best, while at the same time building academic proficiency and reaching grade-level achievement in their second language, English. The development of academic proficiency in a second language (i.e. English) takes a minimum of six years in dual language programs and much longer in other programs for English learners.

So the program should serve English learners first and foremost. In fact, Lau v. Nichols (1974 U.S. Supreme Court decision) requires a meaningful education for English learners. (See Collier & Thomas, 2009, for the strong legal rationale for serving English learners effectively.) Other educational programs provided for English learners are less effective in closing the gap. Dual language education is where the English learners of any one language background belong. And here is where demographics do matter in the decisions that you make for your dual language program. **Choice of the partner language is determined by the total number of students of one heritage language attending your school or school district.** Since over 75% of English learners across the U.S. are of Spanish-speaking background, the majority of dual language programs have Spanish as their partner language, paired with English. Among the other partner languages represented in U.S. dual language schools to be paired with English are Arabic, Armenian, Cantonese, French, German, Japanese, Korean, Mandarin Chinese, Navajo, Portuguese, Russian, and Vietnamese.

Language minority students fluent in English. Now here's where this next decision gets really interesting. Let's take the example of Spanish as the partner language. In most cases the Spanish-speaking students who are not yet proficient in English are enrolled in the program as the group of first priority. After these students are counted, you find that there is still room for more Spanish speakers. The next students that should be invited to enroll are those whose heritage language is Spanish and who are classified as fluent or dominant in English. These Latino students are not served by any special program. They are not eligible for transitional bilingual or ESL services, and yet often they are still working on building their proficiency in English. When tested in English they usually score lower than non-language minority native English speakers—sometimes much lower. When these language minority students who come from a non-English heritage language background enroll in the dual language program, their academic achievement advances much more than when attending monolingual English classes (Collier & Thomas, 2009; Thomas & Collier, 2002, 2009; Thomas, Collier & Collier, 2010). With time, they too close their achievement gap when tested in English, and they develop deeper academic proficiency in English than they would in a monolingual English class. In addition, they connect to their heritage language and culture through the program. They have the opportunity to develop pride in their bilingual/bicultural identity and to assist the community with their newfound bilingualism (C. Sizemore, personal communication, November 19, 2011).

In Figure 4.1 we have used the sociolinguistics term *language minority* to refer to students who come from a non-native-English-speaking background. The term language minority refers to all those who have a language other than English in their family from the last couple of generations. In the sociolinguistic context of the U.S., English is the majority language, so all other languages in relation to English are referred to as "minority languages." This research term, identical

Figure 4.1

Educational Reform
Through Dual Language Programs

Language Minority Students			
English learners (ELLs/LEPs)	L1 dominant, typically below 25th-30th percentile when tested in English	**Served** but present remedial ELL programs are **ineffective**	Need full gap closure rather than half closure
Language minority but not classified as ELL	L1 dominant or L2 dominant or bilingual or fluent only in English	**Not served** by present remedial ELL programs	Need full gap closure rather than partial closure
Non-Language Minority Students			
Native-English speakers	Students in poverty (low SES) attending Title I programs; Special education	**Served** but present remedial programs are **ineffective**	Need greatly improved achievement and gap closure
	Mainstream and gifted students	**Served** and present programs are **effective**	Need improved achievement to reach full potential

Copyright © 2004-2012, W.P. Thomas & V.P. Collier. All rights reserved.

to the term "partner language," implies that partner languages are in danger of not having equal status with English within the broader society. For this reason, dual language programs work to create more of an equal status between the two program languages, thus transforming majority-minority interrelationships. When the term language minority is used by sociolinguists, it can refer to many possible levels of proficiency in the student's two languages. For example, language minority students may be just beginning to acquire English, or they may be fluent in two languages orally but not in writing, or they may have deep oral and written proficiency in the two languages, or they may be monolingual in English. All of these possibilities represent potential enrollees in the dual language program.

Native English speakers. How about native English speakers in a two-way dual language program? They have a valued role in each two-way class. Some two-way Spanish-English programs count the Latinos who are proficient in English (language minority but not English learners) as native English speakers. For research reasons, we separately analyze the scores of language minorities who are not classified as English learners, but for programmatic and funding reasons, they may be counted as native English speakers. In other words, native English-speaking students recruited for the class may include Caucasians, African Americans, Latinos, and students of other ethnic backgrounds who are native English speakers. We have found that students in poverty served by Title I programs, those with special needs, and those who are identified as gifted all benefit greatly through participation in the dual language classroom (to be illustrated in the research findings in Chapters 5 and 6). These students may reach their full potential without compromising their English language development and with greatly increased academic achievement as measured in English. And in the dual language program they have the added benefit of developing academic proficiency in another language, strengthening cognitive development, and becoming cross-culturally competent, ready to navigate in a multilingual world.

A challenge that schools face in making enrollment decisions for the two-way dual language program has been the programs' popularity among well-educated middle class families. As soon as the program is underway and the initial "bumps" of the implementation process are smoothed out, many English-speaking parents, some of whom may have inspired the decision to begin the program, put pressure on the school for their children to be admitted. To maintain balanced classes of roughly equal numbers of English speakers and partner language speakers, as specified in the definition of two-way dual language education, it is often necessary to institute a lottery for admission to the English-speaking half of the class. Of course this frequently leads to a need to open more dual language classes and schools to meet the growing demand. The bottom line, though, is for the dual language program to serve the English learners well, because it holds the greatest promise for academic, linguistic, and sociocultural success for this most "at risk" group. **English learners should represent at least half of the two-way dual language enrollment, because they are the group with the greatest needs and largest achievement gap.** If the demographics favor 1/3 – 2/3 as the balance between the two language groups, that is still considered a two-way program.

Immigrants whose home language is not the partner language. There is still one more group to consider. Some immigrant families of a third language background (other than English and the chosen partner language) do request that their children be admitted to the dual language program, because they already understand the value of multilingualism. This is truly a challenging choice for their children, but if there is space in the program and the parents are clear about their commitment, this is also a choice that can work. In advising these parents, we recommend that they find a way for their children to develop literacy in their mother tongue outside of school, since literacy in first language is such an important key to second language success (Cummins, 1991; Freeman & Freeman, 2006; Goldenberg, 2008; Thonis, 1994). Sometimes the parents are well schooled in the heritage language and able to provide this at home. Occasionally, especially in urban contexts, there are community classes to develop oral and written skills in the heritage language as after-school or weekend opportunities.

Enrollment choices for families. Most dual language classes are a strand within the school; that is, there are both dual language and non-dual language classes in each grade. However, when the dual language school is a schoolwide model, then the school and the school district need to create alternatives for those community families that do not choose dual language. This same issue may arise for English-dominant students who arrive at secondary level and enroll in a dual language school after their primary years in an all-English elementary school. Most often another school in the same or a nearby neighborhood is chosen to provide mono-lingual English classes for these families who choose not to place their children in the dual language school. Also, some schoolwide dual language programs are chosen to be magnet schools, serving a larger region than just the neighborhood where the school is located.

Teachers and staff

When the school community and its leadership have envisioned developing a dual language program and the non-English language has been chosen based on the heritage language of the English learners attending that school, the very next step is to identify and hire qualified bilingual staff who are proficient in that language. It's then necessary to maintain appropriate staffing each time that a teacher or staff member leaves the school or retires. When hiring opportunities present themselves, a bilingual coordinator either within the building or at central administrative level can assist with program-specific issues, including the teacher's academic language proficiency levels (with the partner language) as a part of the interview process.

At the same time that bilingually-endorsed staff are being hired, it is very important to incorporate the existing monolingual English-speaking teachers' skills and experience into the plan for success of the dual language program. These teachers may be responsible for the instructional time in English. If that is the case, they will need to have or secure their TESOL endorsement. Dual language principals report that the natural ebb and flow of teacher retirements can also make it possible to retain all English-speaking staff, so none of their present high quality staff needs to be replaced. Since dual language programs are introduced one grade per year, this provides time for natural staff attrition to occur.

Finding qualified bilingually-endorsed staff is often the most challenging task in developing a dual language program, especially in regions of the U.S. that have experienced a recent influx of immigrants with fewer teachers of that minority language group immigrating to that region or qualifying to teach. In contrast, among communities that have been bilingual for some time, such as the southwest U.S. with its Spanish-speaking heritage, there are growing numbers of applicants who are well qualified to serve as teachers in dual language schools. As dual language schools mature and graduate students who have attended the program all the way through school, K-12, these deeply bilingual students, with high academic proficiency in two languages, are beginning to come back to their communities to serve as bilingual teachers. School community leadership often refers to this as "growing our own" bilingual staff.

For the communities without a sufficient number of qualified bilingual teachers, some regions such as the state of North Carolina have recruited teachers from other countries and provided them with work visas. They also train the faculty as they adjust to cross-cultural systems of teaching within the U.S., encounter non-standard dialects of Spanish and other partner languages, and understand the bilingual contexts that have created these programs. The biggest challenge in recruiting overseas bilingual teachers is that they often do not stay for many years, usually because they prefer to return to their own country when their work visa expires. Thus dual language program directors may work hard to help these teachers settle in their new community and adjust to different ways of teaching in U.S. schools (cooperative learning, different systems for disciplining students, interactive discovery learning, and so on), only to lose these teachers in a few years, after spending so much time training them.

In established bilingual communities, another system for recruitment of teachers for the dual language classes is for the school system to transform their remedial transitional bilingual classes into enrichment dual language classes, since these are already staffed with bilingual teachers. This approach has its own issues to be addressed. Bilingual teachers coming from transitional bilingual classes need professional development support to understand some of the major differences in teaching strategies, in the goals of the program, and in classroom heterogeneity.

The reality is that the dual language classes will be much more diverse than transitional bilingual classes, with many variations in language proficiency and academic background among the students with whom the teachers will be working, especially in two-way dual language classes with native English speakers as second language learners. Transitional bilingual teachers have been accustomed to more homogeneous classes of, for example, Spanish speakers of the same age with similar needs, working on reading and writing in Spanish and just beginning to acquire the English language and curricular subjects. A two-way class taught in Spanish requires that the teacher use second language teaching strategies for the English speakers in the class while at the same time continuing challenging grade-level work in Spanish for both language groups. Those strategies will also be required for the Spanish speakers in the class when instruction is in English—and academic language and literacy are often scaffolded even for students learning in their native language. Because of all these differences in teaching requirements between dual language and transitional bilingual classes, these new dual language teachers will need substantial amounts of professional development and in-service training to successfully implement dual language education.

Staff development and instructional practices

Transitional bilingual education compared to dual language education.

Figure 4.2 provides an overview for central administrative staff, the school board, principals, teachers, and the community to grasp some of the major differences between transitional bilingual classes and dual language classes. The first contrast in Figure 4.2 points out that monolingualism in English is an outcome of transitional bilingual classes, whereas multilingualism is the celebrated goal of dual language classes. Transitional bilingual programs emphasize using the students' first language for a portion of the instructional time for two to three years to help students meet grade-level standards in the language that they know best. But as they work in English during the remainder of the time, their first language is phased out as soon as possible. Students get the clear message that their language is not valued and English is what matters most. Furthermore, they are placed in a class in which they are isolated from native English speakers, and students know they are perceived by their English-speaking peers as not capable of learning at the level of native English speakers.

This perception is reinforced by the second contrast in Figure 4.2, subtractive versus additive bilingualism, a sociolinguistic phenomenon that occurs in bilingual environments throughout the world (Lambert, 1975, 1984). Subtractive bilinguals are encouraged to gradually lose their first language as they acquire the second language, and they tend to do less well in school as the curriculum gets more complex. This happens because cognitive development in first language is stopped too early. Research on the relationship between primary language and cognition says that children must continue developing thinking skills in first language nonstop until at least age 12. Additive bilinguals continue developing cognitively in

Figure 4.2

Why Dual Language Education?

Remedial Education: Transitional Bilingual and ESL Only	Enrichment Education: Dual Language
Monolingualism	Multilingualism
Subtractive	Additive
For English learners only (remedial program)	For English learners, language minorities, native-English speakers (mainstream program)
Short-term K-2 or K-5	Long-term Ideally K-12 or PK-12
Minimal achievement (1/2 or less of gap closed)	High achievement (full gap closure)
Cognitive development slowed/limited	Cognitive development continued/enhanced
Minimal English proficiency	Full proficiency in English plus another language
Teaching more often traditional, directive	Teaching must be learner-centered
Extra teachers, extra costs	Costs similar to mainstream, except for startup

Copyright © 2012, W.P. Thomas & V.P. Collier. All rights reserved.

their first language as they acquire the second language, and the result is cognitive advantages, including greater flexibility in thinking and problem solving. Additive bilinguals deeply proficient in both languages typically outscore monolinguals on all types of school tests (Baker, 2011).

The third contrast in Figure 4.2 represents a dramatic difference between the two program types. Transitional bilingual classes are designed as a separate program, exclusively for English learners. While attending these classes, the students are segregated from the English mainstream, and both students and staff often perceive the program as remedial in nature. In contrast, **dual language classes are**

the mainstream, but taught through two languages rather than one. Dual language classes include all students who want to participate, and the teachers work on grade-level academic learning through the two languages, leading to students' academic giftedness after several years in the program, especially on measures of creativity, problem-solving, and divergent thinking (Baker, 2011; Bialystok, 1991, 2001; Díaz & Klingler, 1991; Tokuhama-Espinosa, 2003). Students are truly proud to be enrolled in the program, because they know they are doing something different that is profoundly challenging. They are also more consciously aware of their bicultural identity and able to handle diverse contexts.

Another contrast is that transitional bilingual classes are designed for the short term, with students attending for two or three years and then "exited" into the English mainstream. Upon exit, students typically have reached half gap closure in their second language, as measured by a norm-referenced curricular test in English (Collier & Thomas, 2009). This narrowed gap does not continue to close after exiting, and the gap may increase with continued years in the English mainstream. Dual language classes are designed for at least PK-8 and ideally should continue throughout the high school years, as well. In this long-term scenario, by Grade 8, dual language students can completely close the gap on norm-referenced tests in both English and the partner language. With full gap closure comes full cognitive development in both first and second languages. As previously discussed, students who receive transitional support in their first language for only Grades K-2 experience potential cognitive slowdowns, since they are no longer continuing their first language cognitive development at school during the important developmental period of ages 8-12. This is an example of subtractive bilingualism, which yields results that are inferior to those of the additive bilingual classroom.

The last two contrasts in Figure 4.2 are typical of separate, extra classes when compared to the monolingual English mainstream classes. Since dual language classes become the mainstream, teaching is rigorous and learner-centered, equal to any other mainstream class. Teaching in transitional bilingual classes can and should be equally strong, but in the past, researchers found that bilingual teachers in separate, segregated classes often did not keep up with the pace of the English mainstream, instead engaging in "watered-down" instruction. This encourages achievement gaps to develop.

Then there is the cost. Separate, remedial programs are always more costly, because they require extra teachers. All types of bilingual programs have the extra expense of preparing and purchasing materials in two languages and providing specific ongoing professional development, but this is a manageable extra cost, within a typical school district budget that receives Title I, Title III and other federal monies. Personnel costs are about 2/3 to 3/4 of the total budget in a typical school district, so extra teachers for ESL/TBE supplementary classes increase the budget much more than materials costs. To be cost-effective, dual language programs can use the same student-teacher ratio that exists within the English mainstream, and thus not over-extend the budget with many extra teachers needing to be hired. In Figure 4.10 at the end of this chapter, we provide another, more detailed overview of the contrast between transitional bilingual and dual language schooling for staff developers to use when training bilingual staff, as well as for educating the community.

Criteria for effective dual language schooling. Figure 4.3 provides a summary of the criteria that we have discussed so far for effective two-way and one-way dual language classes. These points were first summarized by Kathryn Lindholm-Leary, a major researcher in the field of dual language education (Lindholm-Leary, 1990, 2001, 2009). Included in this list are the non-negotiables and other typical characteristics of dual language classes that dual language researchers have found to be crucial to program success. "Focus on the core academic curriculum" emphasizes the importance of maintaining grade-level work through both languages, just like any English mainstream class working through the medium of only one language. This is not easy for the teacher, since each class contains students with varying proficiency in the two languages of instruction. But using sheltered instruction to support second language acquisition and knowing the grade-level curriculum, dual language teachers can create unique and exciting lessons that stimulate both language and curricular content acquisition across all subject areas.

"Quality language arts instruction in both languages" emphasizes the importance of formally developing each language through explicit language arts instruction across the domains of listening, speaking, reading, and writing. Thematic lessons integrate curricular subjects, to link the content directly to the world the students know outside of the classroom. At the same time, dual language teachers need to have explicit language arts objectives planned and embedded in the thematic material, as they help students develop both their first and second languages through meaningful lessons across the curriculum. Metalinguistic awareness and teaching for transfer across the two languages are also crucial components of explicit language arts instruction in a dual language classroom.

Another important principle for dual language classes listed in Figure 4.3 is "promotion of positive interdependence among peers and between teachers and students." This refers to the power of peer tutoring that takes place along with instructional guidance and mentoring between the teachers and students. Cooperative learning is a crucial dynamic within all dual language classrooms, for it is through the interactions among peers, with the instructional task at hand as the focus, that natural second language acquisition takes place. During the instructional time and tasks in English, the native English speakers are modeling English. The modeling takes place as students discuss a project or read a book together. Likewise, modeling of the partner language is the charge of students proficient in that language, during the designated instructional time. The students are crucial peer teachers of each language. The peer teaching is not focused on explicit language lessons, but on the academic and social life within the classroom and the language needed to fully participate. As the students and teachers negotiate and problem-solve complex curricular tasks together, the stage is set for natural language acquisition to take place.

Of course the last two criteria on the list in Figure 4.3 are desirable for any school program. High-quality instructional classroom and support personnel are key to making the dual language program effective. That means the teachers must be fully licensed to teach the grade level(s) and subject(s) they are teaching, they must be

---

Figure 4.3

Criteria for Effective Two-Way and One-Way Dual Language Education

- A minimum of six years of bilingual instruction

- Focus on the core academic curriculum

- Quality language arts instruction in both language

- Separation of the two languages for instruction

- Use of the partner (non-English) language for at least 50% of the instructional time and as much as 90% in the early grades

- An additive bilingual environment that has full support of school administrators, teachers, and parents

- For two-way classes, a balanced ratio of students who speak each language (for example, 1/2 and 1/2 or 1/3 and 2/3)

- Promotion of positive interdependence among peers and between teachers and students

- High-quality instructional personnel

- Active parent-school partnerships

Copyright © 2004-2012, V.P. Collier & W.P. Thomas. All rights reserved.
Adapted from Kathryn Lindholm-Leary, 1990.

---

fully trained in second language teaching methods (bilingual/TESOL certification), and they must be fully academically proficient in the language(s) through which they are teaching. We will discuss the last criterion in this list, "active parent-school partnerships," at the end of this chapter.

Figure 4.4 summarizes five major required elements and instructional strategies for two-way and one-way dual language classes that we have summarized throughout this and the previous chapter. The first two points, language distribution and separation of the two instructional languages, are decisions made as the program is being designed. It is crucial for all teachers to be in agreement and to be consistent in carrying out these pillars of the program design as planned and agreed upon. The remaining three strategies are key instructional practices for all dual language classrooms: integrating language and content, active/discovery/inquiry learning, and cooperative learning. Teachers must be well trained in the skillful and intentional use of these basic instructional practices so crucial to the success of dual language education (Cloud, Genesee & Hamayan, 2000; Freeman, Freeman & Mercuri, 2005; Soltero, 2004).

Figure 4.4

Instructional Strategies in Two-Way and One-Way Dual Language Classrooms

- **Language distribution** follows the chosen program model. In a 90:10 model, 90% of the instructional time is in the partner (non-English) language during the first one to two years of the program, gradually moving toward 50:50. In a 50:50 model, alternation of the language of instruction is done by teacher, time, or subject, with equal instructional time given to each language.

- **Separation of languages:** The teacher speaks exclusively in the language of instruction. (However, young children in Grades K-1 may respond in their language of choice. After two years of L2 development, children are expected to use only the language of instruction.)

- **Sheltered instruction:** The integration of language and content instruction, where teachers use scaffolding/sheltering strategies to make content comprehensible and to support all students in participating.

- **Active/Discovery learning:** Students are actively engaged for meaningful purposes in inquiry-based learning.

- **Cooperative learning:** Language minority and language majority students work together in a structured and intentional way to complete instructional tasks.

Copyright © 2002-2012, V.P. Collier & W.P. Thomas. All rights reserved.

Two-way distinctions. There are some special characteristics of two-way dual language education that distinguish this integrated model from one-way dual language classes. As stated in the previous chapter, while we advise school districts to work with the demographics found in each school community and create the best program for all the students who choose to enroll, there are several reasons to encourage native English speakers to enroll in the program, whether represented in the student body or coming from outside the neighborhood. Two-way classes bring the greatest mix of students, leading to the largest program effect sizes and highest level of achievement of any school program that I, Wayne, have ever seen in 40 years of conducting school program evaluations. The dream of a true multilingual, multicultural citizenry can only be realized when we bring our children together to teach each other.

Figure 4.5 illustrates some of the special features that are somewhat unique to two-way. The stimulus of the two language groups coming together to teach each other leads to favorable and highly supportive cross-cultural exchanges that benefit both groups as they learn to work cooperatively together. It changes the status relations between groups, lessening the effects of majority-minority differences, as well as the effects of the socioeconomic divide. English enjoys such a high status world-wide that it is quite difficult to create an equal status between the two languages. However, in a two-way program, the partner language becomes valued and respected—gaining equal status within a two-way program in a very special way,

Figure 4.5

Program Characteristics of Two-Way Dual Language Education

- Integrated schooling, with native English speakers and language minority students learning the curriculum through each others' languages

- High expectations and high outcomes in student performance in a challenging curriculum delivered through two languages lead to the perception among stakeholders that this is a gifted program

- Equal status of the two languages achieved to a large extent, creating self-confidence among language minority students and an additive bilingual context for both language groups

- Healthy parent involvement among both language minority and native-English-speaking parents for closer home-school collaboration

- Instructional approaches:

    Language taught through academic content

    Balanced literacy approaches

    Cooperative learning

    Interactive, discovery learning

    Cognitive complexity found in all lessons

Copyright © 2004-2012, V.P. Collier & W.P. Thomas. All rights reserved.

because it receives equal instructional time with English (and in a 90:10 program even more time in the early grades). This is especially true when the partner language does not share equal status outside the classroom in the larger school community. The English speakers become aware of the importance of the partner language when they see how much it is used in other countries and how widespread and valuable the partner language is. This changes the relationship between the two language groups in the class, leading to an additive bilingual context for both groups. Trust, respect, partnerships, and even lifelong friendships may form across the cultural groups represented in the class. As one program graduate said, "The bilingual classes changed my life!" because as an Anglo American, she continues to have widespread social contacts across cultural groups in her adult professional and personal life.

In contrast to these advantages of two-way dual language classes, there can be potential problems with segregated bilingual classes, especially the remedial form of bilingual schooling labeled transitional bilingual education, as illustrated in Figure 4.6.

To avoid these potential negative perceptions and the possible break in cognitive and linguistic development that English learners might experience in isolation from native English speakers, it is important for a one-way dual language program to enroll all students who wish to attend, including those of the same heritage who are fluent in English. When the program is taught as equal to the English mainstream—with challenging thematic lessons taught through both languages—and students are clear that their heritage language is a crucial component of the program that will be continued for many grades and used throughout all subjects in the curriculum, then they take their studies in two languages seriously. Over time, they can develop pride in their bilingual/bicultural identity and heritage, and value both maintaing their native language and developing complete proficiency in English (Christian & Genesee, 2001; Cummins, 2000b; Hélot & de Mejía, 2008).

Figure 4.6

Potential Problems with Segregated Bilingual Classes

- The sociocultural context of schooling may not be transformed. For example, negative perceptions of bilingual classes may remain, fostering discrimination and prejudice toward language minority students.

- Social distance from second language peers may remain, making it hard to change majority-minority relations in school.

- When teachers are the only model of second language for instruction, second language acquisition is less efficient. Peer models of second language are important to the process of second language acquisition and raise the cognitive level of language use and learning.

Copyright © 1996-2012, V.P. Collier & W. P. Thomas. All rights reserved.

Community advocacy

Parents from both language groups are an absolutely essential key to planning, promoting, and maintaining high quality program implementation. They are primary partners with the school, and they must be ready and willing to meet the challenges that come with developing and maintaining a dual language program. Well-educated English-speaking parents are often the initiators of a two-way model because they realize the advantages of multilingualism and multiculturalism and want this for their children. Yet educators must be clear from the beginning that the program cannot serve only the English-speaking community. A recently arriving immigrant group may include many skeptical parents who place English development above all school activity and can see no benefit to their children attending school in any language other than English. So a first step is to organize meetings for parents who speak the partner language in order to guide them through the truths and promises that their children can benefit greatly from the dual language program.

Convincing parents. The initial year of the program can be the most challenging in convincing parents, because there must be sufficient enrollment to fill at least two classes at preschool and kindergarten level, and parents are often unsure at the beginning when they have not seen this form of schooling in action. Once families become knowledgeable about dual language, then they become advocates and should be invited to share their testimony as to the challenges and successes of their children and family in the program. Some attrition from the program can be expected year to year (because of families who need to move to other locations) as each succeeding grade is added; so to ensure that there is at least one full class by Grade 5, it is best to start out with two classes as a minimum. Thus, preparing both parent groups to enroll and support their children in that first year is very important to the implementation and longevity of the program.

Reasons to develop two languages from kindergarten on. Figure 4.7 provides a rationale for English-speaking parents to consider enrolling their children in the dual language program. This list emphasizes points that foreign language educators make when they choose to convince parents that middle or high school is much too late to introduce their children to a language other than English. Furthermore, this list illustrates experiences that additive bilinguals have in a dual language program. Native English speakers are additive bilinguals, as speakers of the majority language. A second language is acquired by students at no cost to their English, knowing that their language, heritage, and identity are secure and important to their education. Their English will not be compromised. Acquiring a second language is going to provide intellectual and cognitive advantages and will enhance their cross-cultural awareness.

Figure 4.7

Advantages of Developing Two Languages During the Elementary School Years

- Has a positive effect on intellectual growth

- Enriches and enhances a child's cognitive development

- Leaves students with more flexibility in thinking, greater sensitivity to language, and a better ear for listening

- Improves a child's understanding of his/her native language

- Gives a child the ability to communicate with people she/he would otherwise not have had a chance to engage with

- Opens the door to other cultures and helps the child understand and appreciate people from other backgrounds and countries

- Gives the child a head start in language requirements for college/life

- Increases job opportunities in many careers where knowing another language is an asset

- Increases competiveness in the political, business, and educational communities

Copyright © 1996-2012, V.P. Collier & W.P. Thomas. All rights reserved.

Professional opportunities. Participating in a K-12 dual language program will also generate additional job opportunities for students because they are bilingual, biliterate, and possess a cross-cultural sensitivity that is not an outcome of monolingual educational programs. In interviews that I, Ginger, conducted in 1989 with graduates of my daughter's bilingual class, I found that as adults, all 20 (nine Latinos, two African Americans, nine Anglo Americans) were using their bilingualism within their professional occupations, and many were earning a higher salary because of their bilingual, biliterate and cross-cultural abilities (see Figure 4.8).

The Prism Model. At the meetings for parents who speak the partner language, the most important points to emphasize first are the dramatic cognitive benefits and academic success that their children will experience through fully developing two languages in the dual language classes, as compared to being schooled in the monolingual English classes. Especially important is that all families understand that dual language is the only model that can promise full proficiency in two languages, including the academic proficiency needed to be successful in all content areas. Our first book (Collier & Thomas, 2009) has several figures in Chapter 4 that are crucial to use for informing immigrant and language-minority parents about the research foundations of a dual language program. In that chapter, our theoretical foundation for explaining the rationale for dual language education is illustrated through the *Prism Model*. When linguistic, cognitive, and academic development are provided nonstop for students in both their first and second languages, within a bicultural context that is warm and emotionally supportive, then students excel in school. The figures in Chapter 4 of that book illustrate the complex process of first and second language acquisition; the relationship between the two languages; additive and subtractive bilingualism; the intimate, interwoven nature of cognitive development with continuous use of first language until at least age 12; and thus the crucial support that parents provide when using the family language(s) for cognitive development at home.

Figure 4.8

Case Study Conducted by V.P. Collier, 1989:
Interviews with 20 Graduates of Two-Way Bilingual Education
(9 Latinos, 9 Anglo Americans, 2 African Americans)

Academic achievement: All graduated with bachelors degrees and several with masters degrees. Five double-majored in Spanish plus another subject, and three others majored in Spanish.

Use of Spanish/English: All succeeded academically in English. All maintained native-like proficiency in oral Spanish, and 15 of 20 demonstrated high proficiency in written Spanish. All have used both languages for professional and personal purposes.

Occupations: Majority are teachers. Most have chosen social service occupations that require bilingual skills. Native English speakers have chosen to work with language minority communities in U.S. to assist with access to U.S. institutions and services.

Bicultural acculturation: All have extensive social networks with speakers of both languages from a wide variety of cultural backgrounds.

Attitudes toward bilingual schooling: All expressed positive attitudes toward their bilingual schooling experience. "Opened us to a whole new world ... it changed our lives!"

Copyright © 1989-2012, V.P. Collier & W.P. Thomas. All rights reserved.

English learners' achievement in dual language compared to English learners' submersion in the English mainstream. The most dramatic findings from our research that may be used to enlighten parents who speak the partner language are presented in Figure 4.9 here. This figure presents the lowest and the highest achievement we have seen for English learners, summarizing from all of our research findings of the past 28 years. The bottom red line demonstrates the achievement of English learners whose parents chose to enroll them in the English mainstream from the beginning of school with no special support from an ESL or bilingual teacher—what we refer to as submersion (see Figure 2.4). These students started in all-English in preschool and continued in mainstream English classes, and when tested on the norm-referenced test (Stanford 9) in English, they were on

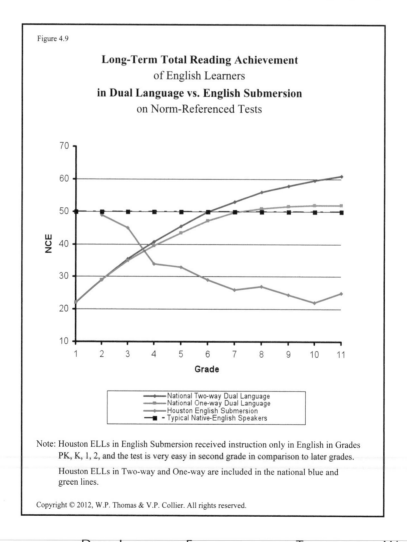

Figure 4.9

Long-Term Total Reading Achievement
of English Learners
in Dual Language vs. English Submersion
on Norm-Referenced Tests

Note: Houston ELLs in English Submersion received instruction only in English in Grades
  PK, K, 1, 2, and the test is very easy in second grade in comparison to later grades.

  Houston ELLs in Two-way and One-way are included in the national blue and
  green lines.

Copyright © 2012, W.P. Thomas & V.P. Collier. All rights reserved.

grade level in second grade, after four years of all-English schooling. But by fourth grade, only two years later, the lack of cognitive development in their first language began to influence their test scores as the cognitive complexity of the test increased with each succeeding grade level. By high school years, among those who received no special bilingual/ESL support, there were only a few students left to be tested; staff stated that the majority of these students had quit school.

In contrast, the top two lines in Figure 4.9 are English learners who received a dual language curriculum through English and their native tongue. These students in one-way and two-way dual language classes outscored native English speakers in English in their high school years. These lines represent average achievement, meaning that half of these students score even higher than this level. All three of these solid lines in the figure represent students who started school with no proficiency in English.

Parent advocacy. After the initial registration in the dual language program and the bilingual classes have achieved stability in enrollment, it is very important for parents from both language groups to participate actively in recruiting new parents to the program. They become the most important advocacy groups, knowledgeable and confident that this way of schooling their children is profoundly exciting and transformative. Parents who speak the partner language may want to organize meetings that serve their special needs, especially if they are a new immigrant group within the community.

Summary

In conclusion, Figure 4.10 presents a summary of the major differences between remedial transitional bilingual and enrichment dual language schooling, and an overall summary of the points in this chapter. This overview can be used to organize issues for staff development sessions, as well as for parent informational meetings. This rationale for quality, enrichment dual language schooling emphasizes the major characteristics that make the difference. In the following chapters, we will demonstrate the remarkable achievement of students participating in dual language education.

Figure 4.10

Upgrading Transitional Bilingual Education (TBE) for English Learners to Dual Language Education (DLE) Programs For All Students

Factor	TBE	DLE
Program Intent	Monolingualism in English for English learners	Bilingualism for all
Program Nature	Subtractive, remedial, separatist, isolating	Additive, enrichment-oriented, integrated
Students Participating	English learners only	English learners, language minorities, native-English speakers
Program Length	Early-exit: usually 2-3 years Late-exit: 5-6 years	Ideally K-12
Language Status	High status for English; less emphasis on L1 or on English learners' culture	High status for English and L1; emphasis on L1 and L2 cultures
Prism Model: Academic Facet	Minimal academic development in L1 leads to below-grade-level in L2	Grade-level achievement in all subjects in L1 and L2
Prism Model: Cognitive Facet	L1 cognitive development stopped at school before completion around age 12	Full L1 and L2 cognitive development
Prism Model: Linguistic Facet	Minimal L1 academic development leads to minimal L2 proficiency	Full L1 and L2 proficiency development
Prism Model: Sociocultural Facet	Social and cultural support while in TBE but only short-term	Full sociocultural support throughout all grades of DLE
Instructional Objectives	Content and language lessons sometimes separated	Content and language objectives combined in every lesson
Classroom Lessons	Code-switching and translation allowed	Monolingual lesson delivery; translation de-emphasized; bridging and transfer required
Teaching Strategies	Cooperative learning sometimes used	Cooperative learning required
	Scaffolding sometimes used	Scaffolding required
	Multi-sensory approach sometimes used	Multi-sensory approach required
Classroom Language Models	Teacher only	Teacher and peer students
Instructional Grouping	Homogeneous	Heterogeneous
Student Self-esteem	Can be negative	Bicultural identity and elevated self-esteem
Program Outcomes: Achievement	Short term: Content achievement gains in English; test scores to 25th-35th percentiles	Short term: Content achievement gains in L1 and L2; scores to 50th percentile (and above) in L1 and L2
	Long term: half of achievement gap closed in English	Long-term: all of achievement gap closed in L1 and L2
Program Outcomes: Attendance	Below average attendance	Increased attendance
Program Outcomes: Dropout Rate	Higher eventual dropout rate	Lower eventual dropout rate
Operational Costs: Teachers	Sometimes higher if extra teachers are hired for TBE as a separate program	No extra cost, except for startup; same teacher-student ratio as in mainstream
Operational Costs: Materials	Higher than English-only (but small impact on total budget)	Higher than English-only (but small impact on total budget)
Opportunity Costs (needs not met as EL population increases)	Huge future costs in lost productivity from half gap closure and resulting lower SES	Large future cost savings from full gap closure, increased productivity, increased SES

Copyright © 2009-2012, W.P. Thomas & V.P. Collier. All rights reserved.

Reflections from the Field

Much of the research on the most effective methods for instructing children who speak a language other than English but who are limited in their English proficiency suffers from one of two limitations: limited empirical data or rudimentary theoretical conceptualization. The team of Collier and Thomas overcomes these common limitations. Dr. Wayne Thomas is a master of analyzing "big data" on the academic progress of hundreds of thousands of linguistically diverse children in different types of instructional programs across the U.S. Dr. Ginger Collier is a master of "big theories" about how and why the language of instruction affects the academic development of linguistically diverse students. Together, they both prove and explain why dual language should be the U.S. standard for all students living in a trans-formed world.

James J. Lyons

Policy Attorney and Consultant
Arlington, Virginia

Chapter Five: Astounding Effectiveness— The North Carolina Story

Like other states, North Carolina has experienced a tremendous increase in numbers of new immigrants during the past two decades, the large majority from Mexico and Central America. As of 2011, the total number of English learners in the state was approximately 154,000, representing 240 languages other than English, with Spanish the most common language spoken. As these families have arrived and impacted public schools, the ESL content programs for English learners have improved with each year. Initiatives from the North Carolina Department of Public Instruction have included intensive SIOP (Sheltered Instruction Observation Protocol) training for both ESL and mainstream teachers in many districts. The state ESL directors have also led many other professional development initiatives that focus on serving English learners more effectively (Lachance & Marino, 2012). Several years ago, the state of North Carolina contracted with the authors of this book to research the effectiveness of two-way dual language programs, one of the models created to address the achievement gaps between English learners and students whose home language is English. In this chapter, we are reporting the results of our long-term findings to date.

Development of dual language education in North Carolina

The story of how two-way dual language programs came to exist in North Carolina public schools is an unusual one. Approximately 25 years ago, a foreign language initiative came from the governor's office, calling for elementary schools to develop programs to teach foreign languages, beginning in kindergarten. After experiments with expansion of Foreign Language in the Elementary School (FLES) classes across the state, several successful bilingual immersion programs were developed for native English speakers, in which the standard grade-level curriculum is taught through a foreign language for a portion of the instructional time. These programs were created in response to the state initiative, while at the same time they provided the beginnings of operational experience with dual language concepts for educators across the state.

The first two-way dual language program welcoming English learners as well as native English speakers began in 1997 at Collinswood Elementary School in the city of Charlotte. This Spanish-English dual language program enrolled approximately half Spanish speakers and half English speakers. The program grew grade by grade, becoming a schoolwide model, and included a continuation plan for middle school. A forward-thinking Latina educational leader, María Petrea, the principal of Collinswood, monitored the program's development, did benchmark testing, hired a biliteracy trainer and a parental outreach staff member to work with both the Latino and English-speaking communities, and worked to ensure that this became a model program in North Carolina. After several years of successful implementation, Collinswood Elementary School organized and hosted the first state conference on dual language education, and the seeds were planted for other schools in the state to consider this two-way model.

Meanwhile, there were several actions at the state level that have made North Carolina a possible model for other states to follow in developing dual language education. In the NC Department of Public Instruction, the foreign language and ESL offices were organized under a single director, which fostered greater collaboration between the two offices not often found in state departments of education. With the support of a foreign language initiative from the governor's office, the state successfully applied for and received a FLAP grant (Foreign Language Assistance Program) from the U.S. Department of Education. This funding provided stimulus money for individual school districts to start more bilingual immersion programs for native English speakers and for the state to develop clear guidelines and consistent implementation criteria for these programs. These efforts included curricular standards for study in the non-English languages as well as initiating training for English-medium and partner language teachers. The large majority of these programs initiated with the FLAP grant were designed only for native English speakers, but some of the schools recognized that they also needed to serve English learners in these classes. As a result, seven school districts now have well established two-way dual language programs, with more being developed each year.

Using the FLAP grant, the state organized and sponsored professional development for administrators and teachers in these programs in the form of bilingual summer institutes. These summer institutes brought consistency in common terminology, teaching methods, administrative practices, and curricular standards for North Carolina bilingual programs. **The state directors and attendees agreed that programs mainly for English speakers would be labeled "immersion," while integrated programs for both English learners and English speakers would be labeled "two-way dual language,"** following common program labeling. In just a few schools, one-way programs were developed for English learners and they are labeled "developmental bilingual." Throughout the state of North Carolina, as of 2011 there are now 51 schools that have a program in which students are taught the curriculum through a foreign language for a significant portion (at least 50%) of the instructional time. Spanish is the most common partner language, with other languages being Mandarin Chinese, German, French, Japanese, Greek, and Cherokee. Native speakers of Spanish, Chinese, French, and Cherokee are included in these programs.

Thomas and Collier research in North Carolina

Our longitudinal research is focused on the seven school districts with two-way dual language classes that have reached at least third-grade level, the initial grade level for state testing. Eleven of the 12 two-way dual language schools in this study are Spanish-English, with one Mandarin Chinese-English class in one school. Only Collinswood and Oaklawn in Charlotte are schoolwide programs (K-8). The others are strands representing a portion of the total school, with several dual language classes for each grade level. The schools are located in urban, suburban, and rural areas, and the programs serve many students of low income background. Each school has grown their dual language program grade by grade, starting with kindergarten and adding a new grade with each proceeding year. Two of these schools now have established preschool dual language classes.

North Carolina dual language implementation practices

Non-negotiables. These NC two-way programs have adhered to the three non-negotiables of dual language: a K-12 commitment, separation of the two languages for instruction, and a minimum of 50% of instruction in the non-English language (Rogers, 2009). All of these schools except one have planned a strong continuation of the dual language program at the middle school level, and four middle schools have already received the first classes of dual language students from their elementary feeder schools. The first classes of dual language students in Charlotte schools have now graduated from high school.

Equitable balance of student groups. These schools have worked very hard to meet the theoretical ideal for two-way programs by maintaining a balance of English learners and native English speakers throughout the grades, with close to an equal number of native speakers of each language. In addition to English learners, several of the schools also have enrolled significant numbers of African American native English-speaking students in the dual language classes, as well as students of low socioeconomic status (as measured by percentage of students receiving free and reduced lunch), making these classes an interesting experiment in closing the academic achievement gap for these historically low-performing groups. In the research figures that follow we will report on the achievement of each group separately.

The high achievement of each separate dual language group is one of the reasons that we have used the words "astounding effectiveness" for the title of this chapter. As a program evaluator for four decades, I, Wayne, do not typically use the word "astounding" when referring to school program effects. The effect sizes associated with these dual language schools are consistently the largest and most pervasive across all participant subgroups of any I have seen in my professional career.

Professional preparation of North Carolina dual language teachers. We believe that part of the reason for such large effect sizes is that these programs have been well implemented and focused on fidelity to the program design in their structures and systems of support. In particular, all of the staff of these dual language programs have received a significant amount of training in SIOP/TWIOP (Two-way) strategies, and four schools have literacy coaches trained in dual language techniques who serve as ongoing, in-house staff developers. Many of the dual language teachers and administrators have attended a variety of summer institutes and national conferences for ongoing professional development and networking. Five of these programs maintain a close connection with the teacher education faculty at a local university in their region, and some serve as sites for internships and student teachers (e.g., East Carolina University, UNC-Chapel Hill, UNC-Charlotte, UNC-Greensboro).

Team teaching. Because at this time in North Carolina there are very few qualified bilingual teachers who are fully proficient in both languages, most of the dual language classes are team-taught by an English-speaking teacher (ESL trained) paired with a bilingual teacher who is academically proficient in the non-English language. In most of the schools, these two teachers have their own classrooms located close to each other, and they teach two classes each day, as the students are accustomed to alternating between the two teachers each day. For example, in Greene County schools, the classrooms are labeled "English world" and "Spanish world." When the students are inside each classroom, they are immersed in that language, as the teacher uses only that language for instruction, curricular materials, cultural experiences, visuals around the room, and displays of student work. As an added support the classroom is print rich and filled with support text and materials in the world language of their instruction.

Biliteracy development: Learning to read in partner language first. Almost all of these mature dual language programs have chosen to teach all students to read in the partner (non-English) language first (sequential biliteracy), because they have found that this works best for both the English learners and the native English speakers. The teachers and principals have faithfully followed the advice given to them by dual language trainers that both language groups should stay together and teach each other. Thus in kindergarten almost all of these Spanish-English schools are following the 90:10 model with 90% of the instructional time in Spanish. After both language groups have a good foundation in reading and writing in Spanish, they introduce English reading, again keeping the students together. Some switch to 50:50 in first grade (equal time in each language) and others wait until second or third grade. Two schools have chosen simultaneous biliteracy, starting instruction in kindergarten with the 50:50 model.

Popularity of North Carolina dual language programs

These dual language programs are so well liked by English-speaking parents that every school has a waiting list for the English speakers hoping to attend, and eight of the 12 schools enroll English-speaking students by lottery because they have such a long waiting list. For most of these schools, Latino parents have become strong advocates of this program model with each additional year of program maturity. Three of these schools have had to work hard to recruit Latino students since the schools are not located in a neighborhood with larger Latino demographics. Five programs are district-wide magnet programs, with half of each dual language class reserved for native Spanish speakers and enrollment by lottery for the native English speakers who choose to attend.

Most of these schools enjoy great support at the central administrative level, and these administrators acknowledge that more dual language schools could be developed if they were able to find and/or develop more qualified bilingual staff. These schools have relied heavily on Visiting International Faculty programs to find qualified bilingual teachers recruited from Spanish-speaking countries. In the future, they hope to "grow their own" teachers by hiring their graduates who choose to join the teaching profession.

Our Thomas and Collier research findings in North Carolina schools

In this chapter we are presenting our latest findings from the second year of this five-year longitudinal study of two-way dual language schools in North Carolina (Thomas, Collier & Collier, 2010). These results are very similar to the first-year findings (Thomas & Collier, 2009). While the research figures that follow are cross-sectional results from School Year 2008-2009 (cross-sectional means examining the school records of all students attending the dual language classes in one school year—i.e., one sample of students at one point in time), these results provide a glimpse of our potential longitudinal findings (following the same students over several years), because almost all of the students attending the dual language classes in the upper grades have been in the dual language program since kindergarten. Those interested in the study can follow the results of our longitudinal findings in future years on the NC Department of Public Instruction website at *http://www. esl.ncwiseowl.org/resources/dual_language/*.

North Carolina schools in our 2010 study. The data sample analyzed consists of all available information on students in the school districts operating at least one dual language program for at least four years, which includes Chapel Hill-Carrboro City: Carrboro Elementary (PK-5), Glenwood Elementary (K-5), and McDougle Middle School (6-8); Charlotte-Mecklenburg: Collinswood Language

Academy (K-8), Oaklawn Language Academy (K-8), and West Mecklenberg High School (9-12); Chatham County: Siler City Elementary (K-5); Durham County: Southwest Elementary (PK-5); Greene County: Snow Hill Primary (K-2), West Greene Elementary (3-5); and Winston Salem/Forsyth County: Ashley Elementary (K-5). In Johnston County, the Selma Elementary dual language program has now reached third grade and is being included in the next year's analyses. The Mandarin Chinese-English program at Glenwood Elementary has been the only two-way program taught in a language other than Spanish.

The K-8 dual language schools in Charlotte-Mecklenberg County are school-wide models, while the other county programs are strands with at least one dual language class per grade, and most have two or more dual language classes per grade. Most of these programs do a good job of maintaining an equal number of English learners and native English speakers at each grade level, honoring the importance of integration of the two language groups in a two-way class.

Participation in dual language classes by ethnicity. The principals and program directors of NC dual language schools have worked diligently to inform all groups within their school communities about the potential advantages of the dual language program, so that parents of all ethnic groups may choose to enroll their children in the program, and non-participating staff and school community members can understand and advocate for the program. Figure 5.1 illustrates the balanced representation of ethnic groups within the two-way dual language classes in comparison to those students not attending dual language classes. Whites, Asians, and multi-racial students participate in dual language classes in approximately the same percentages as their group's percentage of non-participants. African American students are underrepresented in dual language, while Hispanic students make up more than a third of the dual language participants.

Description of analyses. The following analyses describe the Reading and Mathematics achievement of all students from the six NC school districts that had at least one school implementing dual language classes. To be included in the study, these students had attended school for at least 90 days of the instructional year 2008-2009 and took the standard North Carolina state End-of-Grade Reading or Mathematics test.

In the first research figures presented here for grades 3, 4, and 5, three groups are compared:

> Group 1: Students attending dual language classrooms in dual language schools (red columns, labeled "DL schl & DL class");

Figure 5.1

Race/Ethnicity of Students in
DL Programs (and Not in DL)

Race/Ethnicity	Students In DL	Students Not in DL
Hispanic	33.8%	16.5%
White	31.8%	36.8%
African American	24.0%	38.5%
Bi- or Multi-racial	7.0%	4.7%
Asian	3.4%	3.3%
Native American	0.0%	0.2%
Total	100.0%	100.0%

Copyright © 2010-2012, W.P. Thomas and V.P. Collier. All rights reserved.

Group 2: Students not in dual language classrooms but in the same school as the dual language students (green columns, labeled "DL schl & non-DL class"); and

Group 3: Students in the same school district but not in a dual language school (blue columns, labeled "Non-DL schl & class").

In these elementary school grades, we were able to provide two non-dual language comparison groups (Groups 2 and 3) to make the comparison more informative by comparing dual language students to non-dual language students both in their school and in other district schools, and thus controlling for some potential between-school effects.

For Grades 6-8, we show only two comparisons because the dual language schools are schoolwide models.

Group 1: Students attending dual language classrooms (red columns); and

Group 2: Students in the same school district but not in a dual language school (blue columns).

In addition, we have analyzed the data by several subgroups of interest. Each figure focuses on one subgroup at a time. For the first four figures, we divide these subgroups into three mutually exclusive groups with subcategories. **This study includes very large numbers of students (a total of 85,662 students for School Year 2008-2009).**

(1) English learners (N = 9,834);

(2) Language minority students who were never classified as English learners (N = 6,635); and

(3) Non-language minority native English speakers:

      a. Whites (N = 33,095);

      b. African Americans (N = 32,155); and

      c. Other (N = 3,943).

(See Appendix B in Collier & Thomas, 2009, for an explanation of the Thomas-Collier *Test of Equal Educational Opportunity*, comparing these three groups.)

Two additional analyses focus not on ethnicity, but on students of low socio-economic status, as well as students with exceptionalities. The first analysis compares students participating in free and reduced lunch programs who attend dual language classes (the red columns) to students participating in free and reduced lunch programs who are not attending dual language classes (the green columns). The second comparison is between students with exceptionalities who attend dual language classes (the red columns) and students with exceptionalities who are not attending dual language classes (the green columns). In summary, the subgroups are presented in the following order in the figures: English learners, language minority students who were never classified as English learners, African American students, White students, students participating in free and reduced lunch programs, and students with exceptionalities. Reading achievement for each subgroup is presented first, followed by mathematics achievement for each subgroup.

Reading achievement. The four figures 5.2-5.5, illustrating Reading achievement on the NC End-of-Grade tests, present the results for each of the four student groups listed above ("Other" not included) to compare students attending dual language and not attending dual language classes. After these four disaggregations of the data by ethnicity/English proficiency, in Figure 5.6 we examine the same data by socioeconomic status, as measured by those students who participated in the free and reduced lunch program.

As can be seen in each of these figures, English learners, language minority students fluent in English (mostly Latinos), Whites, and African Americans in dual language classes (the red columns in these figures) are all out-performing their comparison groups not in dual language. In fact, **by the middle school years and sometimes sooner, two-way dual language students, regardless of subgroup, are often at least one grade level ahead of their comparison group. These findings in favor of dual language are both statistically and practically significant.**

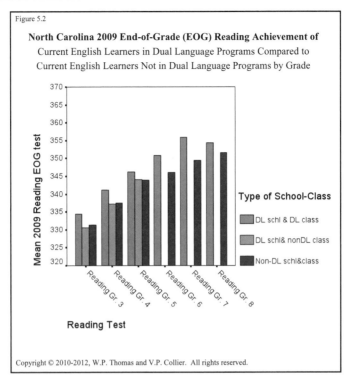

Figure 5.2

North Carolina 2009 End-of-Grade (EOG) Reading Achievement of
Current English Learners in Dual Language Programs Compared to
Current English Learners Not in Dual Language Programs by Grade

Mean 2009 Reading EOG test

Type of School-Class

☐ DL schl & DL class

☐ DL schl& nonDL class

■ Non-DL schl&class

Reading Test

Copyright © 2010-2012, W.P. Thomas and V.P. Collier. All rights reserved.

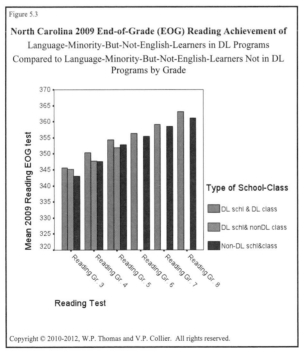

Figure 5.3

North Carolina 2009 End-of-Grade (EOG) Reading Achievement of
Language-Minority-But-Not-English-Learners in DL Programs
Compared to Language-Minority-But-Not-English-Learners Not in DL
Programs by Grade

Mean 2009 Reading EOG test

Type of School-Class

☐ DL schl & DL class

☐ DL schl& nonDL class

■ Non-DL schl&class

Reading Test

Copyright © 2010-2012, W.P. Thomas and V.P. Collier. All rights reserved.

Chapter Five—Astounding Effectiveness: The North Carolina Story   73

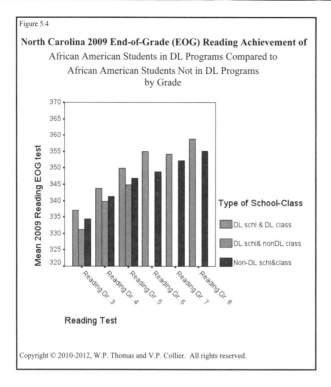

Figure 5.4

North Carolina 2009 End-of-Grade (EOG) Reading Achievement of
African American Students in DL Programs Compared to
African American Students Not in DL Programs
by Grade

Copyright © 2010-2012, W.P. Thomas and V.P. Collier. All rights reserved.

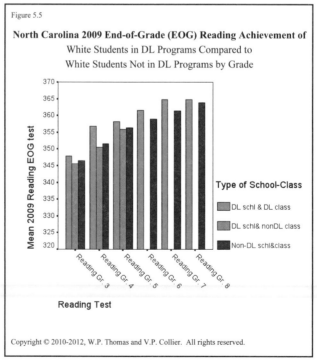

Figure 5.5

North Carolina 2009 End-of-Grade (EOG) Reading Achievement of
White Students in DL Programs Compared to
White Students Not in DL Programs by Grade

Copyright © 2010-2012, W.P. Thomas and V.P. Collier. All rights reserved.

DUAL LANGUAGE EDUCATION FOR A TRANSFORMED WORLD

In this case, statistical significance means that the observed differences are not likely to be the result of chance, and thus likely to reflect real differences between scores of dual language and non-dual language students, if other variables have been accounted for. Practical significance means that the observed differences between dual language and non-dual language students are large enough to represent a significant fraction of a standard deviation (effect size) and thus have both practical and operational importance for "real world" decision-making.

Socioeconomic status. When examining all achievement data from the state of North Carolina, both current English learners and African American native English speakers show very large achievement gaps when compared to White native English speakers. Furthermore, the large majority of English learners (80.7%) and African American students (64.5%) are of low socioeconomic status—that is, many of the students in these two groups are participating in free and reduced lunch programs. However, **when English learners and African American students of low socioeconomic status participate in dual language programs, they score very strongly higher (in terms of practical significance) in EOG Reading in all grades, compared to English learners and African American students not attending dual language programs. The dual language program seems to strongly counteract the negative impact of low socioeconomic status on school achievement.**

This continues to confirm our findings from other studies that we have conducted that strong, effective dual language programs can overcome or reverse much of the negative effect of low socioeconomic status on school achievement (see Figure 6.10 in Collier & Thomas, 2009; Thomas & Collier, 2002).

Exceptionalities. Our next finding on students with exceptionalities (special education) is tentative but promising. Since students

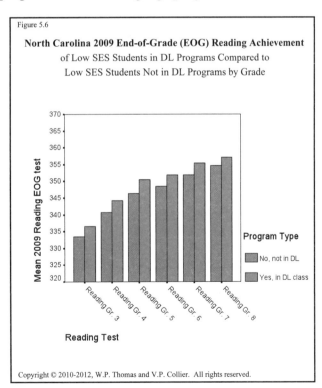

Figure 5.6

North Carolina 2009 End-of-Grade (EOG) Reading Achievement
of Low SES Students in DL Programs Compared to
Low SES Students Not in DL Programs by Grade

Copyright © 2010-2012, W.P. Thomas and V.P. Collier. All rights reserved.

with exceptionalities are a unique group of students with special needs, we analyzed these students separately to investigate the impact of two-way dual language programs on their achievement. Many parents wonder if dual language classrooms are appropriate placements for students with special needs. Genesee has confirmed that the voluminous research from Canada on this question answers "Yes"—that is, whatever students are experiencing, each group does significantly better in a bilingual class than in a monolingual class (Genesee, Paradis & Crago, 2004).

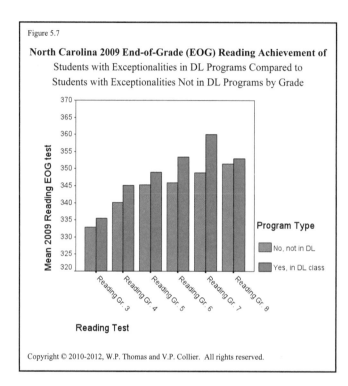

Figure 5.7

North Carolina 2009 End-of-Grade (EOG) Reading Achievement of Students with Exceptionalities in DL Programs Compared to Students with Exceptionalities Not in DL Programs by Grade

Copyright © 2010-2012, W.P. Thomas and V.P. Collier. All rights reserved.

In this study, we examined only the special needs students who were administered the NC End-of-Grade tests rather than an alternative test. There were a small number of students tested within this category, a total of 86 students in our 2008-2009 analyses, with the majority in the exceptionality categories of specific learning disabilities and speech-language impairment. But as can be seen in Figure 5.7, these students in dual language classes outperformed their peers not in dual language, confirming findings from other researchers' analyses (Bruck, 1982; Genesee, 1987; Genesee, Paradis & Crago, 2004; Lindholm-Leary & Genesee, 2010; Lindholm-Leary & Howard, 2008). The eighth grade column in Figure 5.7 is not generalizable, because it represents only five students. But even with smaller sample sizes, the scores of the dual language special needs students in Grades 6 and 7 are both statistically and practically significant.

Our findings on students with exceptionalities are consistent with our overall conclusion that schooling through two languages in a well-implemented dual language program greatly benefits all students, whatever their circumstances and their educational needs. However, additional analyses with larger groups will be necessary to strengthen this tentative finding on students with exceptionalities/special needs.

Mathematics achievement. To illustrate achievement in one other subject area, we have chosen to report on mathematics as a subject to compare with the results of the Reading tests. In all of our analyses over the years, we have found that the Reading measure of each test is the most challenging for students beginning in Grade 3 and beyond. This is because the items on the Reading test combine and integrate curricular materials from all the subjects into one test. Thus, students tend to score higher on the subtests that isolate each subject area, such as Mathematics, Social Studies, or Science, than on the Reading measure. But for university or college admissions, the standardized tests (e.g., the SAT or ACT) examine both Reading and Mathematics. Since we want all of our students to have an equal chance of pursuing studies beyond Grades K-12, in our analyses we provide a look at achievement data on both of these measures. Generally, we find that students tend to score higher on the Mathematics tests than the Reading test, as illustrated in the findings of this study. But interestingly, in North Carolina the dual language students of all backgrounds outscored the non-dual language students on the Mathematics test, too.

Overall, the higher achievement of all dual language students on both the Reading and Mathematics tests is statistically significant and practically very significant. Mathematics achievement for each group (English learners, African Americans, Whites, students of low socioeconomic status, and students with exceptionalities) is illustrated in Figures 5.8-5.12.

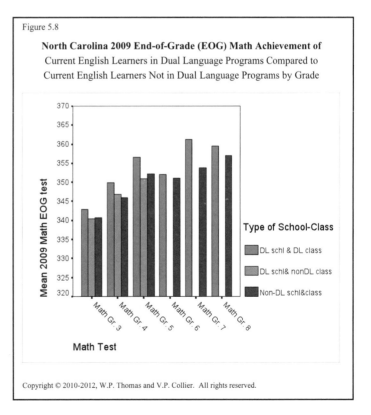

Figure 5.8

North Carolina 2009 End-of-Grade (EOG) Math Achievement of Current English Learners in Dual Language Programs Compared to Current English Learners Not in Dual Language Programs by Grade

Copyright © 2010-2012, W.P. Thomas and V.P. Collier. All rights reserved.

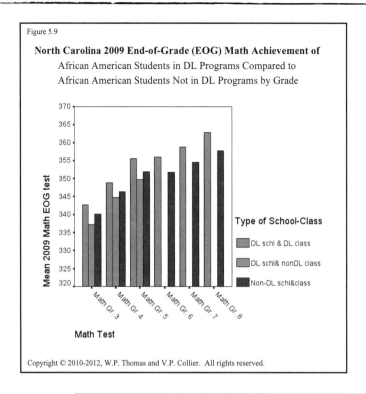

Figure 5.9

North Carolina 2009 End-of-Grade (EOG) Math Achievement of
African American Students in DL Programs Compared to
African American Students Not in DL Programs by Grade

Copyright © 2010-2012, W.P. Thomas and V.P. Collier. All rights reserved.

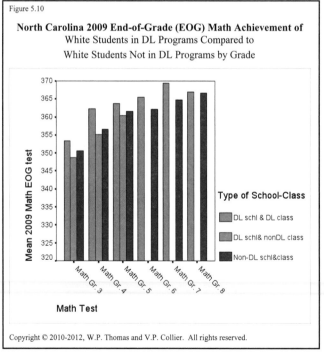

Figure 5.10

North Carolina 2009 End-of-Grade (EOG) Math Achievement of
White Students in DL Programs Compared to
White Students Not in DL Programs by Grade

Copyright © 2010-2012, W.P. Thomas and V.P. Collier. All rights reserved.

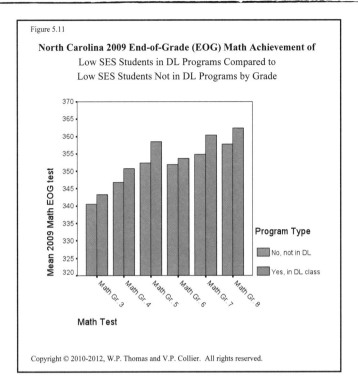

Figure 5.11

North Carolina 2009 End-of-Grade (EOG) Math Achievement of
Low SES Students in DL Programs Compared to
Low SES Students Not in DL Programs by Grade

Copyright © 2010-2012, W.P. Thomas and V.P. Collier. All rights reserved.

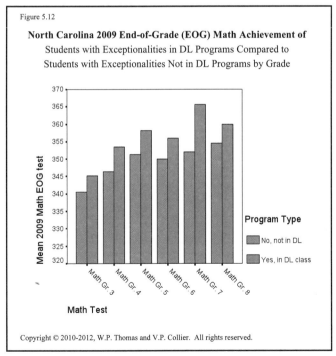

Figure 5.12

North Carolina 2009 End-of-Grade (EOG) Math Achievement of
Students with Exceptionalities in DL Programs Compared to
Students with Exceptionalities Not in DL Programs by Grade

Copyright © 2010-2012, W.P. Thomas and V.P. Collier. All rights reserved.

Chapter Five—Astounding Effectiveness: The North Carolina Story   79

Initial longitudinal analyses. During the coming year following publication of this book, we will be completing the first data analyses that examine this North Carolina data from a longitudinal perspective, following the same students across time. As of now, we have started this process with a longitudinal scatterplot following individual students' performance on the NC test over a one-year period, examining their test scores at the end of third grade and the same students at the end of fourth grade. Scatterplots are quite useful for looking at the distribution of test scores and how student scores change over time. Scatterplots also provide useful information by identifying any outliers (extreme scores that may be inaccurate), as well as for checking on the degree of "straight line" relationship between variables. Figure 5.13 illustrates English learners' achievement on the NC Reading tests at third and again at fourth grade.

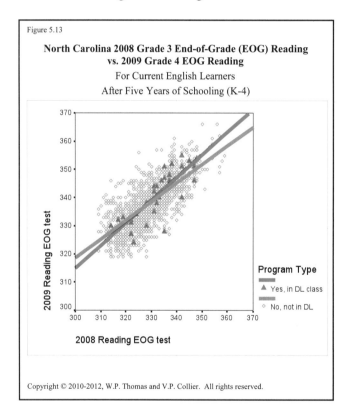

Figure 5.13

North Carolina 2008 Grade 3 End-of-Grade (EOG) Reading vs. 2009 Grade 4 EOG Reading

For Current English Learners

After Five Years of Schooling (K-4)

Copyright © 2010-2012, W.P. Thomas and V.P. Collier. All rights reserved.

The red triangles on this scatterplot represent test scores of English learners who are attending dual language classes, and the green squares represent test scores of English learners in the same school district who are not attending dual language classes. The red and green lines show the best-fitting regression line for each of these two groups.

As shown in Figure 5.13, for current English learners, the relationship between post-test score (2009 Reading as fourth graders) and pre-test score (2008 Reading as third graders) is linear (best described by a straight line), so the multiple linear regression analyses that follow are appropriate. Second, the scatterplot shows that there are no extreme scores (outliers) that might unduly distort the analyses of this data. This also indicates that a multiple linear regression analysis may be conducted validly. Third, the scatterplot shows that the slope of the best fitting line for the dual language students is steeper than the slope of the best fitting line for the non-dual language students, indicating that the dual language students may be scoring significantly higher than the non-dual language students between the end of third grade and end of fourth grade.

A more formal regression analysis confirms that the dual language students scored significantly higher at Grade 4 than the non-dual language students, when the Grade 4 reading scores were adjusted for the Grade 3 reading scores as a covariate. Such preliminary analyses are normally conducted prior to the multiple linear regressions and analyses of covariance for each group of interest, including English learners, Latinos fluent in English, African American students, White native English speakers, and others.

Multiple regression analyses. Now don't stop reading here, because this part gets even more interesting! In education, many variables can influence student achievement. In fact, in quantitative analyses, it is difficult to pin down the precise influences, because so many variables cannot be collected or measured in a quantifiable form. Multiple regression can assist with this process, but it does not answer all questions. In any quantitative study, some but not all of the variables that potentially explain what is going on can be investigated to see how much impact they have on student achievement when the effects of other variables are statistically removed.

The independent variables, examined in Figure 5.14, explain about 52% of the total variation in NC End-of-Grade test scores in this study. That means that almost half of the variation observed is due to other factors, some for which we may not have data. But this figure does illustrate some findings that are statistically and practically significant, reflecting the "unique" effect of each variable listed, when the effects of the other independent variables that have been collected are controlled for in the regression analyses. It also provides information to help the reader interpret the gains per year on these NC End-of-Grade tests.

- North Carolina students' Reading scores typically increase across each grade between Grades 3-8 by 3.7 scale score points per year. This provides a context for interpreting the influence of other variables on achievement because it provides an indicator of the size of "one year's growth" in the following bulleted points. In other words, the effect of each of the variables examined can be roughly compared to an annual gain of 3.7 scale score points for the typical student.

- Across all grades and regardless of school program, North Carolina students of low socioeconomic status (participating in free and reduced lunch) score 4.6 points lower in Reading than students who are not of low socioeconomic status.

- Male students score 1.1 points lower in Reading than female students.

- Each day of missed school attendance is associated with a drop of one-tenth of a scale score point. Thus, a student who misses 10 days of school might be

Figure 5.14

North Carolina 2009 End-of-Grade (EOG) Reading
Multiple Regression Results

Independent Variable (IV) and IV values/levels	B Coefficient (Change in scale score with each change in value of the IV)	Std. Error	T	Sig.
Student SES (Low SES compared to Not-Low)	-4.55	.069	-66.3	<.0001
Student Grade (From grades 3-8)	+3.70	.017	217.8	<.0001
Student Gender (Male scores compared to Female)	-1.07	.058	-18.3	<.0001
No. Days Student Attended School (90-180)	+0.10	.003	29.3	<.0001
Student Has Exceptionality (No compared to Yes)	+6.40	.091	70.0	<.0001
Class Type (Non-DL in DL School compared to DL in DL school)	-2.67	.338	-7.9	<.0001
Class Type (Non-DL in NDL School compared to DL in DL school)	-2.13	.254	-8.4	<.0001
T-C Group (ELLs compared to non-LM Whites)	-10.22	.109	-94.0	<.0001
T-C Group (LM-but-not-ELL vs non-LM Whites)	-1.77	.108	-16.4	<.0001
T-C Group (Non-LM African-Americans compared to non-LM Whites)	-7.56	.076	-99.8	<.0001
T-C Group (Non-LM Others compared to non-LM Whites)	-3.07	.146	-21.1	<.0001
Multiple R for this model = .72		Multiple R squared for this model = .52		

Copyright © 2010-2012, W.P. Thomas and V.P. Collier. All rights reserved.

expected to score one point lower on the Reading test, where a typical year's gain is 3.7 points. In a separate analysis, we found that dual language students attend school an average of three days more per year than non-dual language students.

• On average across all grades, students not in dual language classes scored 2.7 points lower per year than students in dual language classes, when in the same school. On average across all grades, students in non-dual language schools scored 2.1 points lower per year than students attending dual language classes.

• When examining all North Carolina achievement data for this school year (2008-2009) by each group separately, the following patterns were present: English learners scored 10.2 points lower than White non-English learners; African Americans scored 7.6 points lower than Whites; students of low socioeconomic status (SES) scored 4.6 points lower than non-low-SES students; and students with exceptionalities scored 6.4 points lower than students with no exceptionalities. **Since the dual language classes significantly increase student achievement for all of these groups, the findings of this study strongly favor dual language classes for all students**.

Summary of findings and conclusions

In summary, results from all of these North Carolina analyses indicate that all groups of students benefit greatly from dual language programs. English learners and African American students especially strongly benefit. As part of the North Carolina experience, this chapter ends with a Thomas and Collier interview that was reprinted from a publication written for NC educators. The interview focused on the implications of the Thomas and Collier research on dual language education in NC. From a different perspective, the following quote illustrates the pride and commitment of the North Carolina Department of Public Instruction directors who facilitate initiatives and professional development support for NC programs for English learners:

> The final, resounding message North Carolina sends is that we are *all* language teachers. Up-to-date, standards-based, data-driven approaches to initiatives are essential for accelerated academic language acquisition. English learners are members of our communities and schools, and we have profound ethical and legal responsibilities to ensure equity and equality for all students in our state.... North Carolina is proud of its initiatives. We hold fast to the notion that public K-12 education is for *all*. As we continue to grow and change, we aim to hold ourselves to the highest of state and national standards for best practices in English learner education.

> (Lachance & Marino, 2012, p. 22)

An Interview with the Authors—

In this publication written for North Carolina educators...
Drs. Thomas and Collier share the educational implications of their research on dual language programs. This interview is adapted and reprinted with permission from *ESL Globe, 8*(1), Spring, 2011. It was conducted by Nancy Swisher, Editor, and Dr. Toby Brody, Editor-in-Chief of this online newsletter of NC State University.

1. *In Chapter One of your first book in this series (Collier & Thomas, 2009) you discuss the large achievement gap between native speakers and English learners and state: "In the U.S, current and former English learners with unmet needs are no longer a small minority. As a nation, we cannot afford continuation of current education practices that have produced this large gap, at the risk of under-preparing a large segment of our citizenry for the 21st century." Just how wide is that gap and what are some current trends in bilingual and ESL instruction that can help close it?*

When English learners are first tested in English using the standard curricular measure, such as a state test or a norm-referenced test, their performance on the reading subtest (which generally measures Reading across the curriculum) is what we use in our research as an indicator of their academic achievement levels in second language. After approximately 2 to 3 years of schooling in the U.S. when schooled only in English (e.g., minimal ESL pullout), we find that English learners on average score around the 10th -12th percentile on the Reading subtest. That means the English learners are scoring about 1.2 national standard deviations below native English speakers when tested in English. Since the norm group of native English speakers averages at the 50th percentile (grade-level performance), that's a huge gap.

The most effective English learner programs we've seen, dual language programs, are capable of closing the large gap (1.2 national standard deviations) at the rate of about 0.2 national standard deviations per year. This means that the strongest programs for English learners will require about six years to fully close the gap. Three-year programs only close half of the gap at best.

Thus current strategies that close the gap in the shortest amount of time possible are found in dual language programs, in which English learners are receiving the curriculum at least half of the instructional time through their mother tongue and the other half in English. English learners enrolled in these programs can fully close the gap in second language in six years if the program is really well implemented, making 1½ years' progress each year (in comparison to the progress of native English speakers on grade level, who only need to make one year's progress to stay on grade level). Dual language schools are being implemented in North Carolina in a number of school districts, and both English learners and native English speakers in these dual language classes are outperforming their peers in all grades in which they are tested (3-8). By middle school they are scoring one grade level above their peers in 6th-8th grade because of the intellectual stimulus of schooling through two languages.

For schools not yet implementing dual language programs, ESL taught through academic content is crucial to accelerate the closing of the achievement gap for English learners, but only the type of primary language support provided by dual language classes closes the second half of the gap.

2. You state that your research shows that dual language programs work best to close the achievement gap. Could you briefly explain why?

Schools implementing dual language programs are committed to transformation of the relationships between groups of students. The cross-cultural context for integrated schooling (e.g., Anglo American, African American, and Hispanic American students acquiring the curriculum through their two languages, Spanish and English) allows for greater creativity in lessons that teach problem-solving across the curriculum from many cross-cultural perspectives. It is a natural context for teaching each other through discovery learning. In the North Carolina dual language schools, there is also a widely diverse socioeconomic mix in each classroom, which leads to students respecting and valuing each other as partners in the learning process, whatever their background. The English-speaking students in dual language classes often perceive the program as an unusual gifted curriculum (the North Carolina schools are so popular that they have to enroll English speakers by lottery), so they are greatly motivated to attend and excel in school. The "prestige" of the program then influences the desire for high achievement among the Spanish speakers, and it's a win-win for all groups.

Also, dual language programs are powerful developers of students' cognitive skills. This important factor enables students to better address the more difficult items on the tests they take, and thus to score higher. They also master the more cognitively demanding aspects of the curriculum. Both of these combine to allow English learners to close the normally unclosed second half of the achievement gap (from 30th to 50th percentiles). For example, in school districts in Texas where students have made it all the way through K-12 dual language classes, the dual language students excel academically, and they have a strong graduation rate and are admitted to four-year universities with scholarship assistance.

3. How long does it take to fully close the achievement gap, and do most existing dual language programs serve students long enough?

It takes an average of 6 to 8 years to fully close the gap. This is also true for native English speakers acquiring the second language, when they are tested on curricular tests in the second language. It is a non-negotiable that dual language programs must continue at least throughout the elementary school years (K-5, and if there is a preschool, then PK-5), and most dual language programs continue into the middle school years, too. Transitional bilingual education (TBE) is a very different type of bilingual program, and in states that have implemented this model, students often receive bilingual schooling for only 2 to 4 years, not enough to fully close the achievement gap in English. A number of states that used to implement mainly TBE are now expanding the dual language model to many schools (e.g., Texas, New Mexico, Illinois, New York), after the longitudinal research has clearly shown the benefits of schooling students through two languages for at least six years and preferably for Grades PK-12.

4. ESL and monolingual English teachers often admonish their students to speak more English at home. Why is this not always a good idea?

Home is the most important context where cognitive development occurs. When children continue to use the language(s) that the parents know best, from birth to at least age 12, they are receiving nonstop cognitive development. Parents are a wonderful source for the stimulation of thinking skills when they talk with their children, such as asking questions, making decisions, discussing daily activities, cooking, shopping, telling stories, sharing family heritage, and so on. When parents use the language(s) in which they are cognitively mature (because they have used their home language(s) throughout their growing up and adult years and cognitive development is not directly connected to schooling, but instead to life experiences), then they are presenting an adult cognitive model to the child and nonstop cognitive development takes place. When parents speak to their children in English and English is not the language in which they are cognitively mature, their children's cognitive development is slowed down.

Research shows that children whose first language use is stopped or slowed down before age 12 may experience cognitive development slowdown, whereas those whose first language is continuously developed through at least age 12 have cognitive advantages. Furthermore, proficient bilinguals (who develop written as well as oral proficiency in both languages) outscore monolinguals on many types of measures—especially in measures of creativity and problem-solving.

5. What are some ways to support students' primary languages in schools, absent a full-fledged dual language program?

Academic content courses in primary language (L1) (taught by foreign language faculty at secondary level), hiring bilingual school staff, using L1 volunteer tutors (including parents, peers, and cross-age tutors), providing books and other resources in L1 in the library and all classrooms, preparing lessons in units that incorporate other languages in a meaningful way (e.g., bilingual storytellers, L1 pen pals across classes or schools through email, journal writing in L1, environmental print in L1 for young readers, show and tell in L1, learning centers in L1), building partnerships with parents to continue L1 cognitive and academic development at home, using the school building for after-school or weekend school taught in L1, encouraging students to contribute articles in L1 to student publications, allowing social use of L1 outside of classes, encouraging extracurricular activities and school celebrations in L1, sending newsletters and school information to parents in L1, providing family math and literacy programs in evenings and weekends in L1 …

6. President Obama has urged Congress to send him a new education law, but with no action by Congress, the U.S. Department of Education is pursuing administrative remedies. What changes would you recommend be included in a future No Child Left Behind law under any administration?

Since the Obama administration supports the idea that a world-class education means acquiring a second language, it makes good sense for federal stimulus funds to be provided immediately for two-way dual language schools (programs that integrate native English speakers with another language group so that they acquire the curriculum through the students' two languages). Towards the end of the Clinton administration, funding was provided for developing two-way dual language programs, so this funding should be restored and increased dramatically, since the educational and research-based case for doing so is much stronger now.

Dual language programs represent an improvement over teaching foreign languages as subjects to native English speakers. Introducing students to foreign language at middle school and high school level for as little as one hour per day is too little and too late. Acquiring a second language naturally through the entire curriculum and throughout the instructional day from the beginning of students' school years is an ideal way to develop deep proficiency in the language while increasing student achievement in both languages. Since English learners also need to close their achievement gap as they master English, these programs are a win-win for both groups.

Another major change that needs to be made by the federal education establishment is to lessen the punitive aspects of the NCLB legislation and allow schools to truly meet students' needs by encouraging discovery learning and creative teaching. And when analyzing test data, rather than emphasizing comparing last year's fourth graders to this year's fourth graders (completely different groups with different needs), they should focus analyses on longitudinal research, following the same students across time. Assessments of student progress and evaluative judgments about program quality should be based on where each student started and how much progress that student has made, year by year.

The advent of emphasis on the Common Core State Standards in instruction will lead to increased cognitive difficulty and complexity in instruction. While this is welcome, the tests that are used to evaluate instruction must be dramatically changed and improved. Tests should be improved so that they become much more than minimum-competency measures of low-level skills (the typical state test). This feature of NCLB has encouraged uninspired, scripted, "teacher-proof," and uninteresting instruction, when we have always needed to engage students at higher levels of cognitive demand in the classroom to help students with much-needed cognitive development. This is especially true of English learners, who must both develop cognitively as much as native English speakers do **and** master the curriculum in a second language (English), a demanding feat.

Since well-implemented dual language programs already emphasize greater cognitive demand in instruction and increased cognitive development in students, these programs are a natural fit for the Common Core instructional emphasis of the near future. In fact, we predict that dual language students will tend to outperform other students from the beginning on Common Core tests when more cognitively complex assessments are used, because properly-implemented dual language programs are already emphasizing cognitive development, and this will be evident in dual language students' scores on the first generation of Common Core assessment results.

The federal government should also pay close attention to recent research showing that bilingualism is quite beneficial for brain development in all humans. These findings also support strong findings from several major meta-analyses and large longitudinal research studies conducted in the past 15 years that support the benefits of bilingualism for all students, not only English learners. Taken together, all of these substantial studies represent a firm foundation for present and future federal policies that would support the states' efforts to encourage dual language programs, and to thus improve education for all their students and also support existing federal initiatives in educational reform nationwide.

In summary, dual language programs are an ideal educational environment for attaining important existing national education goals and for assisting state education reform efforts. They are also an ideal instructional infrastructure for meeting the goals of the new state emphases on Common Core instruction. Substantial research has shown these programs to be effective for all participating groups, especially historically low-scoring groups such as African Americans, Title I students, and English learners. And so we, as well as many other educators, parents, and community members across the country, feel strongly that the federal government should now recognize these factors and immediately take action to provide the necessary financial support for all state and local school districts who are ready to adopt dual language programs as an across-the-board reform of U.S. education. The opportunity for the federal government to provide meaningful and substantial assistance to the states in implementing an educational reform with a proven track record for all students should not be missed or delayed any longer by the current or any future administration in Washington.

REFLECTIONS FROM THE FIELD

Virginia Collier and Wayne Thomas's book, Educating English Learners for a Transformed World, validates and fuels the hard work we have been doing in developing and maintaining our dual language program over the years. Given recent changes in the demographics of our school community and in national attitudes and policies regarding immigration and multilingualism, we find ourselves reflecting on the structure and trajectory of our dual language program. We look forward to Virginia and Wayne's continued work as we face old and new challenges in maintaining a quality dual language program. Their work inspires us and gives us much hope as we support our students and our future.

DIANA PINKSTON-STEWART

BILINGUAL PROGRAM COORDINATOR
EAST SAN JOSÉ ELEMENTARY
ALBUQUERQUE, NEW MEXICO

CHAPTER SIX: MORE DUAL LANGUAGE RESEARCH FINDINGS FROM THOMAS AND COLLIER

Over the past 28 years of our joint Thomas and Collier research, we have conducted many longitudinal evaluations of school programs for English learners, working with 35 school districts in 16 states within the U.S. and including two federally funded studies. Out of this lifelong work, our research figure that many refer to as "The Graph" was first published in 1997, based at that time on over 42,317 longitudinal student records. In addition, the findings of this figure were confirmed and validated by our national study funded by the U.S. Department of Education (Thomas & Collier, 2002). After now having analyzed over 6.2 million student records, and still finding the same general patterns in student achievement, we can confirm that these findings are very generalizable to all regions and contexts of the United States.

This research figure is well known, with many other researchers also confirming the crucial role that primary language plays in schooling English learners. When researchers analyze student achievement data across a number of years and focus on students who are not yet proficient in the majority language of the country when they first begin their schooling, they find patterns similar to those we have found. Research syntheses as well as meta-analyses of many U.S. studies examining long-term English learner achievement in bilingual schooling are summarized and/or analyzed in Collier, 1992; Dolson, 1985; Greene, 1998; Krashen & Biber, 1988; Lindholm-Leary, 2001; Lindholm-Leary & Borsato, 2006; Lindholm-Leary & Genesee, 2010; Lindholm-Leary & Howard, 2008; Ramírez, 1992; Rolstad, Mahoney & Glass, 2005; Troike, 1978; and Willig, 1985.

Along with fellow researchers across the world, we continue to find that the most powerful predictor of language minority student achievement in second language is nonstop development of students' primary language through the school curriculum. For example, research syntheses on bilingual schooling from many other countries include the following: Baker, 2011; Baker & Prys-Jones, 1998; Christian & Genesee, 2001; Cummins, 2000b; Cummins & Hornberger, 2008; Dutcher, 2001; García, Skutnabb-Kangas & Torres-Guzmán, 2006; Hélot & de Mejía, 2008; May & Hill, 2005; Skutnabb-Kangas, Phillipson, Mohanty & Panda, 2008; and Tucker, 1999. As we have shown in the previous chapters of this book, dual language programs uniquely provide this development opportunity for all students when the essential and non-negotiable components are adhered to and implemented well.

Since this research figure is the basic foundation of our work, we have chosen to reprint it here from our first book in this series (Collier & Thomas, 2009), with a brief overview of some of the key points that staff development experts need to understand when training educators—or educating the community— about this figure. In the previous chapter, we focused our review on student achievement patterns on only one state test. In Figure 6.1 we are comparing student achievement in different programs for English learners as measured by norm-referenced tests in English (the students' second language), providing national comparisons across states. For more detailed explanations of this figure, refer to Chapter 5 of Collier and Thomas (2009).

What "The Graph" includes

All solid lines represent English learners:

- of low socioeconomic status, as measured by free and reduced lunch;
- from all major regions of the U.S., including urban, suburban, and rural schools;
- who started kindergarten with no proficiency in English and are followed longitudinally from grades K-12; and
- who received the special program for English learners only during their elementary school years (2-7 years, depending upon the type of program).

The dotted line at the 50th percentile/NCE represents the average performance of native English speakers across the United States (the norm group) on the English Reading test at each grade level.

The direction of program lines is important.

- Flat lines indicate one year of progress in one year's time, the average progress of native English speakers on the English Reading test.
- Lines going up indicate gap closure, with English learners making **more** progress than native English speakers.
- Lines going down mean that the gap is widening, with English learners making **less** progress than native English speakers.

Line 7 (Proposition 227 in California) represents a series of two-year cohorts of English learners tested in the spring of 1998, 1999, and 2000, each two-year cohort beginning in each successive grade. The administration of state tests in California was changed after the year 2000 as a part of standards-based reforms, thus limiting this quasi-longitudinal study to two-year cohorts.

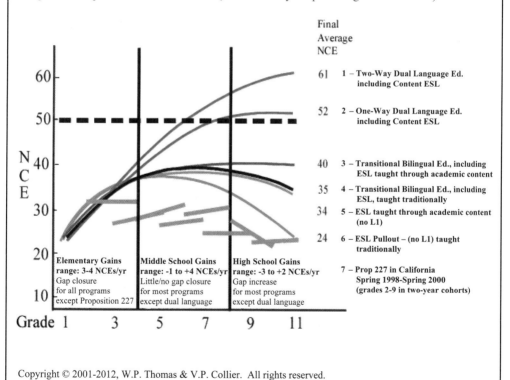

Figure 6.1

English Learners' Long-Term K-12 Achievement in Normal Curve Equivalents (NCEs) on Standardized Tests in English Reading Compared across Seven Program Models

(Results aggregated from longitudinal studies of well-implemented, mature programs in five school districts and in California)

Program 1: Two-way Dual Language Education (DLE), including Content ESL
Program 2: One-way DLE, including ESL taught through academic content
Program 3: Transitional BE, including ESL taught through academic content
Program 4: Transitional BE, including ESL, both taught traditionally
Program 5: ESL taught through academic content using current approaches with no L1 use
Program 6: ESL pullout - taught by pullout from mainstream classroom with no L1 use
Program 7: Proposition 227 in California (successive 2-year quasi-longitudinal cohorts)

Final Average NCE

61   1 – Two-Way Dual Language Ed. including Content ESL

52   2 – One-Way Dual Language Ed. including Content ESL

40   3 – Transitional Bilingual Ed., including ESL taught through academic content

35   4 – Transitional Bilingual Ed., including ESL, taught traditionally

34   5 – ESL taught through academic content (no L1)

24   6 – ESL Pullout – (no L1) taught traditionally

7 – Prop 227 in California Spring 1998-Spring 2000 (grades 2-9 in two-year cohorts)

Elementary Gains range: 3-4 NCEs/yr Gap closure for all programs except Proposition 227

Middle School Gains range: -1 to +4 NCEs/yr Little/no gap closure for most programs except dual language

High School Gains range: -3 to +2 NCEs/yr Gap increase for most programs except dual language

Copyright © 2001-2012, W.P. Thomas & V.P. Collier. All rights reserved.

What "The Graph" is telling us

1. When beginning ESL students are followed across time, comparing their achievement as tested in English by program type, the findings are as follows:

   - differences among student groups are quite small initially (indicating no significant difference among program outcomes in the early years, Grades K-3, of schooling);

   - differences in average student performance become significantly larger in middle school, depending on program model experienced during the elementary school years; and

   - differences in average student performance are very large in high school, depending on program model experienced during the elementary school years.

2. Only dual language programs (with long-term academically and cognitively enriched instruction in two languages, one of which is the primary language of the English learners and the second instructional language is English) allow English learners to score as high as (or higher than) typical native English speakers after 6-8 years, when tested on the English Reading test, which tests curricular mastery in all subjects combined.

3. In the long term, most of the other programs for English learners, both English-plus and English-only, close the first half of the achievement gap, but not the second half. **Only dual language programs eventually close all of the achievement gap**.

4. English learners in all programs appear to do well in terms of gap closure during Grades K-3. (Both school and tests are easier in early elementary school than later on.)

5. Real differences in program outcomes only become discernible after instructional and testing difficulty increase in the late elementary and middle school years. The level of cognitive demand of the tests and the curriculum is much greater in these years.

6. Only dual language programs that provide long-term, enriched teaching of all curricular subjects through English learners' primary language as well as acquisition of English as a second language through all curricular subjects completely close the full achievement gap when tested on difficult English norm-referenced tests that show the full extent of the gap.

7. When tested in English, the highest scoring programs—dual language—are those with less than half or half of the instructional time in English and at least half in the English learners' first language.

8. Enrichment dual language programs in elementary school prepare students for cognitively complex secondary work better than remedial elementary programs.

9. There is a direct and positive relationship between degree of program enrichment and final program outcomes. English learners in remedial, short-term programs score lowest; students in remedial, longer-term programs score better, but do not close the achievement gap; and students in enrichment, longer-term programs score highest, surpassing all students studying monolingually in the English mainstream.

10. All programs for English learners that close more than the first half of the achievement gap in English include first language support.

11. It is easier to close the achievement gap in elementary school than in middle school, and most difficult to close it in high school.

12. More difficult tests, such as the National Assessment of Educational Progress (NAEP) or norm-referenced commercial tests (e.g., Stanford, Aprenda, Terra Nova, Supera, ITBS) show a larger and more accurate achievement gap than most state tests, because of ceiling effects and easier items in the state tests (see Collier & Thomas, 2009, Appendices A and B).

13. Multiple regression analyses (an important part of these studies) show that the program model—especially the amount of first language support—has the strongest effect on achievement for students of low socioeconomic background with no initial English proficiency when they begin schooling in the U.S. Dual language programs provide the most first language support along with nonstop cognitive development for English learners. This is the key to the success of dual language programs.

14. This graph is considered generalizable to many other countries and is used for educational policy making, according to researchers from Africa, Asia, Latin America, Europe, Canada, Australia, and New Zealand. The following syntheses of research from countries around the world refer to our research findings summarized in the graph. Some of these researchers have replicated our studies and found similar patterns of higher student achievement when students are schooled through their mother tongue and a second language: Benson, 2004; Bolton & Baxter, 2011; Bühmann & Trudell, 2008; Coleman, 2007; Cummins, 2000b; Cummins & Hornberger, 2008; Groff, 2005; Klaus, 2003; Magga, Nicolaisen, Trask, Skutnabb-Kangas & Dunbar, 2005; Malone, 2004; May, Hill & Tiakiwai, 2004; Ouane & Glanz, 2011; Pacific Policy Research Center, 2010. In addition, our research findings have confirmed older research studies from other countries with similar results: Cummins, 1981; Dutcher, 2001; Genesee, 1987; Skuttnabb-Kangas, 1979; Spolsky & Cooper, 1977; Swain & Lapkin, 1981, 1982.

We first based Figure 6.1 on research data that we collected from five large school districts. In the 15 years since this figure was originally published, we have continued to conduct program evaluations for many school districts. These studies are requested and paid for by the individual school districts, and therefore the ownership of each study resides with the school district and these are not often formally published. However, with each evaluation of specific programs for English learners, we have continued to assess the pattern of the data from each Thomas and Collier study to determine if it matches our original published Figure 6.1. The remarkable result is that the general pattern is evident in study after study, including the programs investigated in our 2002 federally funded study. In other words, the programs evaluated tend to show outcomes quite similar to each corresponding program type in this figure. That is why the figure is very generalizable across diverse contexts not only in the U.S. but also around the world.

Dual language education in Woodburn, Oregon

One of the school districts that requested that we conduct a five-year longitudinal program evaluation (2001-2005) is located in Woodburn, Oregon. The Woodburn School District has given us permission to publish the results of their study in this book. It provides another outstanding example of dual language schooling in progress, improving with each school year. Four successive superintendents over the past 15 years have committed to the concept of bilingual schooling, resulting in a district-wide K-12 dual language program in all schools in Woodburn. The current superintendent, David Bautista, is an experienced administrator and teacher of dual language education programs and one of the first dual language superintendents in the U.S. Bautista has provided strong leadership in the Woodburn School District for the past two years as superintendent and five years as director of bilingual education. He follows in the footsteps of Superintendent Walt Blomberg, who provided direction for the continuing strategic plan, first initiated in 1997, that led to the districtwide dual language program in all of Woodburn's public schools.

Woodburn is located 30 miles south of Portland, Oregon, and 17 miles north of the state capital at Salem. What defines its uniqueness is the town's diverse population of Hispanic and Russian descent. The three major languages of the community are English, Spanish, and Russian, with a significant percentage of the Spanish-speaking community of indigenous heritage from southern Mexico, with an indigenous language as their first language and Spanish their second language. In the schools and throughout the community, the multicultural heritages of residents are expressed in food, religion, music, dress, language, and the families' deep engagement with and commitment to the schools.

The school district is relatively small (5,400 students), with one preschool center for children of six weeks to five years of age, four elementary schools, two middle schools, and five small high schools developed six years ago with funds from the Gates Foundation. The school population consists of 78% of Hispanic heritage, 13% Caucasian English-speaking, and 9% of Russian heritage. In 2012, 42% of the students enrolled were English learners, and 86% of the total student population participated in the free and reduced lunch program. The innovative K-12 dual language programs that have been created in all of the Woodburn schools for both the Russian-speaking and Spanish-speaking students are not only ensuring academic success but preparing students for a multilingual, multicultural world. The district's goal is for all students to graduate fully literate in two languages, English and either Spanish or Russian.

This program has a unique history. In the early 20th century, members of the Russian Old Orthodox community fled religious persecution in Russia and settled in a number of different locations around the world. By the 1960s, a group of these Russian immigrants chose to move to the Woodburn area. Settlers in this farming community continue to honor their heritage by wearing traditional handmade garments, celebrating Russian holidays, and observing feast days throughout the year. Their churches incorporate hand-painted murals and onion-shaped domes and spires, reflecting the beautiful designs of their heritage.

As the superintendent responsible for all students, including students whose first language is other than English, I feel extremely proud to support the development of biliteracy and cross-cultural programs in Woodburn School District. Assisting students in developing their own language and culture as a part of their studies, knowing that this will reaffirm their identity and their understanding of the multicultural community that we live in, is a humbling experience. The steady advancement of bilingual education in the K-12 Woodburn School District may be an example of academic biliteracy that many educators, researchers, and other members of the community are looking for.

DAVID BAUTISTA, SUPERINTENDENT
WOODBURN SCHOOL DISTRICT
WOODBURN, OREGON

By the 1960s the Woodburn community of Russian-speaking immigrants was of sufficient number that parents requested that the public schools provide bilingual schooling in Russian and English. A heritage language program was established, with some subjects taught in Russian and other subjects taught in English. While the variety of the spoken Russian language of the community is somewhat different from standard Russian, the Russian teachers use standard Russian with students for oral and written work in school, while honoring and respecting the community dialect.

After the Russian community was well established and the Russian bilingual program firmly in place in the schools, immigrants from Mexico as well as Latinos who had previously served as seasonal farmworkers began to arrive and settle in Woodburn, eventually outnumbering the Russian population there. When bilingual classes in Spanish-English were offered to the Latino community, the parents could see the advantages that the Russian families experienced, and after several years, more and more families chose to place their children in the bilingual classes.

As of 2012, the Woodburn school district has 20 full-day kindergarten classes, 15 of which are Spanish-English dual language, two are Russian-English dual language, and three are labeled "English-plus," designed for parents who prefer that their children receive most of their schooling in English. Four of these dual language classes are two-way and 13 are one-way. In the English-plus classes, students receive almost all their coursework in English, with their choice of Spanish or Russian studied as a subject. Two of the dual language elementary schools are 75:25 programs and the other two are 50:50. For literacy development, in the 75:25 classes, every student learns to read first in the non-English language, including the native English speakers. By third grade, all dual language classes are taught 50% of the instructional time in each language. The two middle schools continue the dual language classes, and all five high schools provide some content classes taught in either Spanish or Russian. The Academy of International Studies offers the largest number of courses taught in Spanish or Russian, and in this high school the class of 2012 graduated 95% of the students originally classified as English learners.

Thomas and Collier analyses of student achievement in Woodburn schools

Our study of the dual language program in Woodburn focused on following the students who attended at least 100 days per year between 2001 and 2005. With a student mobility rate of 15% per year, there was considerable student turnover, but the following figures represent those English learners who received dual language services over this five-year period and whose progress we could follow longitudinally. Longitudinal research is more valid and reliable than cross-sectional analyses and more useful for policy and program decision-making. Cross-sectional research, for example, compares fourth graders this year to fourth graders the next year—two completely different groups of students with different instructional strengths and needs. When following the same students longitudinally, we can assess each group's growth by comparing how each group gained relative to its own initial level of achievement.

In the following figures, we examine three groups of students who were administered the Reading subtest of the Oregon State Achievement Test (OSAT) each year. Two of these groups were attending dual language classes—English learners (the blue line) and language minority students classified as fluent in English (the green line, which includes both Hispanic and Russian heritage students). In these initial years of the Woodburn dual language classes, they were mostly one-way heritage language classes, with few native English speakers attending. The red line presents the achievement of native English speakers attending classes taught only in English—the comparison group. Figure 6.2 examines the achievement gains of these three groups from third grade to seventh grade.

Elementary school achievement. Figure 6.2 shows the visual pattern of achievement gap closure for the elementary school cohorts attending the dual language classes. The same data is illustrated in Figure 6.3 in a more detailed table.

At third grade English learners initially experienced a 14.93 point OSAT reading achievement gap with native English speakers in 2001, but were able to close this gap to within 4.94 points by 2005. Since four years separate these testing periods, this amounts to gap closure of about 2.5 OSAT scale score points per year. If this rate of gap closure were maintained, the gap would be completely closed

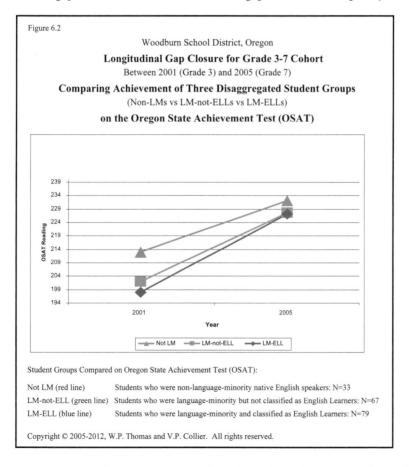

Figure 6.2

Woodburn School District, Oregon
Longitudinal Gap Closure for Grade 3-7 Cohort
Between 2001 (Grade 3) and 2005 (Grade 7)
Comparing Achievement of Three Disaggregated Student Groups
(Non-LMs vs LM-not-ELLs vs LM-ELLs)
on the Oregon State Achievement Test (OSAT)

Student Groups Compared on Oregon State Achievement Test (OSAT):

Not LM (red line)   Students who were non-language-minority native English speakers: N=33
LM-not-ELL (green line)   Students who were language-minority but not classified as English Learners: N=67
LM-ELL (blue line)   Students who were language-minority and classified as English Learners: N=79

Copyright © 2005-2012, W.P. Thomas and V.P. Collier. All rights reserved.

Figure 6.3

Woodburn School District, Oregon

Longitudinal Achievement Gap Summary for Grade 3-7 Cohort
Between 2001 (Grade 3) and 2005 (Grade 7)

Gap Closure for Two Disaggregated Student Groups
(LM-not-ELLs and LM-ELLs)

Compared to Native English Speakers (Non-LMs)
on the Oregon State Achievement Test (OSAT)

Grade 3-7 Cohort	2001 gap with non-LMs	2005 gap with non-LMs	Testing interval	Average gap closure per year in Grades 3-7	Projected total years to full gap closure from Grade 3
English Learners	14.93	4.94	4 years	2.5 points	6.0
LM-but-not-ELLs	11.06	4.61	4 years	1.6 points	6.9

Copyright © 2005-2012, W.P. Thomas and V.P. Collier. All rights reserved.

within two more years. This is in agreement with the achievement gap closure patterns that we have found in other school district analyses that we have conducted of one-way dual language programs (e.g., see Figure 6.1). Likewise, language minority students initially experienced an 11.06 point gap in 2001 but closed this gap to 4.61 points by 2005, four years later. Thus, their projected time-to-full-gap closure from Grade 3 is almost seven years, similar to the achievement of English learners.

It is important to understand that these results mean that Woodburn English learners made significantly more progress each year than native English speakers of the same age. In addition, they achieved this as measured by a test administered in their second language, whereas the native English speakers were tested in their primary language. This indicates that the English learners are mastering the curriculum better because it was presented in both Spanish and English, and the cognitive stimulus of acquiring both languages is also enabling them to outpace the native English speakers who are learning in a monolingual English program.

Likewise, the heritage language students classified as fluent in English, both Spanish-speaking and Russian-speaking, had significant gaps to close in English that were not that different from the English learners. These students also gain greatly from schooling through the partner language and English.

Middle school achievement. Figure 6.4 presents the middle school comparison of the longitudinal achievement gains of English learners, language minority students classified as fluent in English, and native English speakers, for fifth grade through eighth grade. This figure illustrates the continuing greater cognitive demands of instruction during the middle school years, for all groups. It is reasonable to expect that the gap closure rate may slow after the elementary years, and it does from Grade 5 to Grade 8. Analyzing the same middle school data in more detail in Figure 6.5, the annual gain for the older students in the Grade 5-8 cohort is 1.3 OSAT points. This implies that English learners who began participation in the dual language program as middle school students may require longer for full gap closure because of the greater cognitive demand of the secondary years.

Another variable that influences older students' achievement is the amount of formal schooling that they had the opportunity to receive during their elementary school years. However, number of years of missed schooling in the country of origin, before these English learners arrived in the U.S., was not a variable available in this particular dataset.

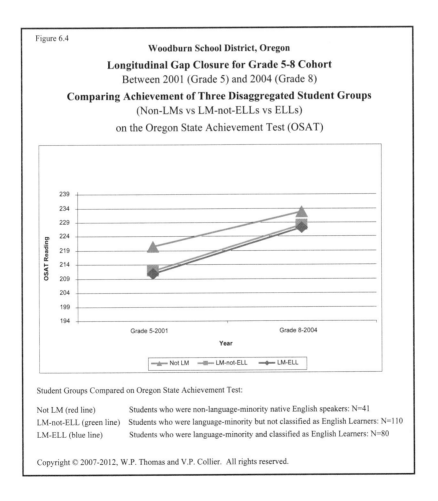

Figure 6.4

Woodburn School District, Oregon

Longitudinal Gap Closure for Grade 5-8 Cohort

Between 2001 (Grade 5) and 2004 (Grade 8)

Comparing Achievement of Three Disaggregated Student Groups

(Non-LMs vs LM-not-ELLs vs ELLs)

on the Oregon State Achievement Test (OSAT)

Student Groups Compared on Oregon State Achievement Test:

Not LM (red line)   Students who were non-language-minority native English speakers: N=41
LM-not-ELL (green line)   Students who were language-minority but not classified as English Learners: N=110
LM-ELL (blue line)   Students who were language-minority and classified as English Learners: N=80

Copyright © 2007-2012, W.P. Thomas and V.P. Collier. All rights reserved.

Figure 6.5

Woodburn School District, Oregon

Longitudinal Achievement Gap Summary for Grade 5-8 Cohort
Between 2001 (Grade 5) and 2004 (Grade 8)

Gap Closure for Two Disaggregated Student Groups
(LM-not-ELLs and LM-ELLs)

Compared to Native-English Speakers (Non-LMs)

on the Oregon State Achievement Test (OSAT)

Grade 5-8 Cohort	2001 gap with non-LMs	2004 gap with non-LMs	Testing interval	Average gap closure per year in grades 5-8	Projected total years to full gap closure from grade 5
English learners	9.69	5.66	3 years	1.34	7.2
LM-but-not-ELLs	8.67	4.76	3 years	1.30	6.7

Copyright © 2007-2012, W.P. Thomas and V.P. Collier. All rights reserved.

Influence of years of missed schooling. Since missed schooling data was not available in Woodburn, Figure 6.6 provides an example from another school district of the strong influence that years of missed schooling in the country of origin can have upon English learners' achievement in the secondary years, as measured by a norm-referenced test. This example comes from our analyses in District E in Thomas and Collier (2002) that provided an outstanding content ESL program for their high school students. We found that on the Reading subtest of the Iowa Test of Basic Skills administered at the 11th grade, English learners who arrived during their secondary years on grade level in their native language were scoring in English (their second language) at the 32nd normal curve equivalent (NCE), which is the 20th national percentile. Those with 3 and 4 years of missed schooling were scoring below the 20th NCE, which is the 8th percentile. (See Collier & Thomas, 2009, Appendix A, for a percentile to NCE conversion table.) As can be

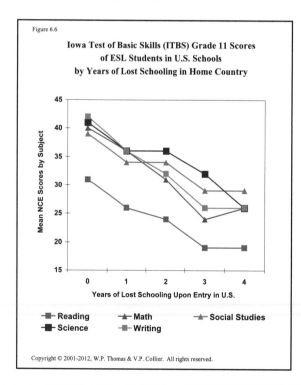

Figure 6.6

Iowa Test of Basic Skills (ITBS) Grade 11 Scores of ESL Students in U.S. Schools by Years of Lost Schooling in Home Country

Mean NCE Scores by Subject

Years of Lost Schooling Upon Entry in U.S.

-■- Reading -▲- Math -▲- Social Studies
-■- Science -■- Writing

Copyright © 2001-2012, W.P. Thomas & V.P. Collier. All rights reserved.

seen in Figure 6.6, each additional year of missed schooling represented a dramatic drop in the achievement of 11th grade English learners in all subtests given in English (reading, math, social studies, science, and writing).

Data displays of individual students. Returning to the Woodburn data analyses, in Figure 6.7 the frequency distributions of OSAT reading scores in Grade 3, compared to the same students at Grade 5, are very instructive. This is another way to display data from state tests, by focusing on the mastery criterion or "cut score" for each grade, with a visual display of the passing rate of a given group, in this case the English learners from the one-way dual language program in Woodburn at the elementary school level. In these displays, to the left of the thick, black vertical line,

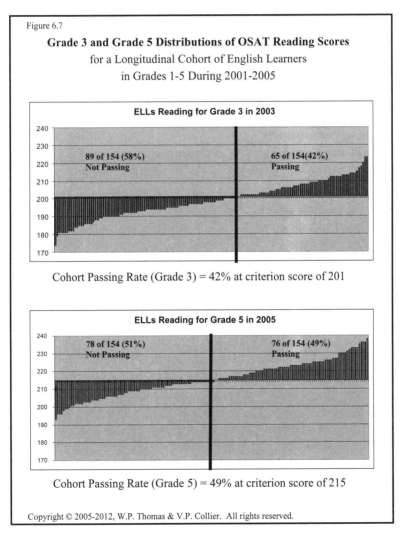

Figure 6.7

Grade 3 and Grade 5 Distributions of OSAT Reading Scores

for a Longitudinal Cohort of English Learners

in Grades 1-5 During 2001-2005

ELLs Reading for Grade 3 in 2003

89 of 154 (58%)
Not Passing

65 of 154 (42%)
Passing

Cohort Passing Rate (Grade 3) = 42% at criterion score of 201

ELLs Reading for Grade 5 in 2005

78 of 154 (51%)
Not Passing

76 of 154 (49%)
Passing

Cohort Passing Rate (Grade 5) = 49% at criterion score of 215

Copyright © 2005-2012, W.P. Thomas & V.P. Collier. All rights reserved.

each thin, descending line represents the score of an individual student achieving below the passing score. To the right of the thick, black vertical line, each thin ascending line represents the score of an individual student achieving above the passing score. For the third grade scores in 2003, the passing score on the Oregon state test was 201, and for the fifth grade (the same students in 2005) the passing score was 215. With all of these English learners' scores displayed together, one can visually see how many students scored above and below the passing score and by how much.

This type of display illustrated in Figure 6.7 is much more useful for pragmatic decision-making than merely knowing that the Grade 3 passing rate for English learners was about 42% and the Grade 5 passing rate for the same group was about 49%. These displays can be used to identify students whose scores are close to the "cut-off" score. We can see in the Grade 3 display that the majority of students not passing were within 10 points of doing so and almost one-third are within 5 points of the passing score. The display also demonstrates the high above-grade-level achievement of some English learners as shown by the lines on the right side of the figure.

Comparing the third-grade display to the fifth-grade display, the same longitudinal group of English learners were able to significantly increase their passing rate from 42% to 49%, even though the Grade 4-5 curriculum is more difficult and the Grade 5 standard for passing is 14 scale score points higher than in Grade 3. An increase in passing percentage for any group indicates that the group is exceeding expected growth rates. For English learners, this means that they are progressing faster than the expected rate of gain between Grades 3 and 5, as defined by the test developers. In other words, Woodburn English learners are closing their achievement gap with native English speakers. In 2012, Woodburn, a school district with 86% of their students of low socioeconomic background and 42% of their students classified as English learners, is successfully graduating the large majority (over 90%) of their high school seniors (D. Bautista, personal communication, June 22, 2012). Many attribute much of this success to the K-12 dual language program now in place in all Woodburn schools.

Classroom-level data collection. We would like to provide one more example from our research in another Oregon school district of the pragmatic usefulness of displays of frequency distributions by scores on a state test, in Figures 6.8 and 6.9. These two figures are from our Thomas and Collier (2002) federally funded study. The examples are from one dual language Spanish-English third-grade class at Grant Community School in Salem, Oregon. Figure 6.8 shows the achievement of individual native English speakers on the reading measure of the Oregon state test, and Figure 6.9 illustrates the native Spanish speakers' achievement on this same test, with the "cut-off" score of 201. We encourage classroom teachers to display your own class data from the results of your state test in this way, to illustrate the

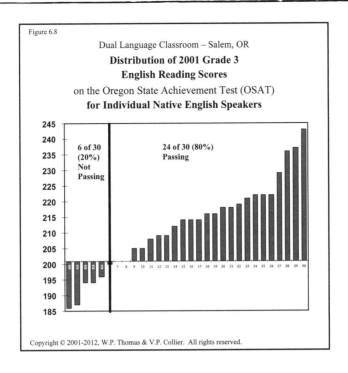

Figure 6.8

Dual Language Classroom – Salem, OR

Distribution of 2001 Grade 3
English Reading Scores
on the Oregon State Achievement Test (OSAT)
for Individual Native English Speakers

6 of 30
(20%)
Not
Passing

24 of 30 (80%)
Passing

Copyright © 2001-2012, W.P. Thomas & V.P. Collier. All rights reserved.

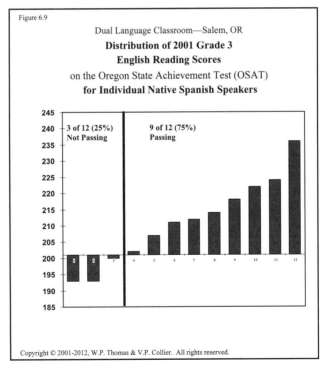

Figure 6.9

Dual Language Classroom—Salem, OR

Distribution of 2001 Grade 3
English Reading Scores
on the Oregon State Achievement Test (OSAT)
for Individual Native Spanish Speakers

3 of 12 (25%)
Not Passing

9 of 12 (75%)
Passing

Copyright © 2001-2012, W.P. Thomas & V.P. Collier. All rights reserved.

For additional visuals of our Thomas and Collier research findings, we encourage you to read the first book in this series (Collier & Thomas, 2009). Chapter 6 includes more findings from two-way and one-way dual language Spanish-English classes in Houston, Texas, and one-way dual language French-English classes in Madawaska, Maine, illustrating above-grade-level achievement in English as students move into the middle school years.

true achievement of your students. The steps for creating a frequency distribution with classroom data are outlined at the end of this chapter.

Summary

This overview of some of our Thomas and Collier research findings, with examples from one of our evaluation studies in Woodburn Public Schools, provides a window into the complex process of analyzing longitudinal data, and the powerful impact that it can have on school decision making. With the results of our 2001-2005 study and follow-up studies, Woodburn policy makers have been able to make a case for implementing Spanish-English and Russian-English dual language schooling in all schools throughout the school district. In Woodburn and many other school districts where evaluations have been conducted, it is truly astounding how well dual language students are doing as they are schooled through their heritage language and English. Educators always add the cautionary words that "we are a work in progress," as the needs of the community continue to be met through continuing refinements in the innovations implemented.

Classroom data collection:
Creating a frequency distribution of test scores

1. For one subtest (e.g., Reading), start with individual test scores in a spreadsheet (e.g., Excel) with one student per row.

2. Sort the scores from lowest to highest.

3. Select the option to construct a chart, and select the chart type as "column" to create a frequency distribution of scores.

4. Specify the point where the X-axis crosses the Y-axis as the value of the "cut score" or passing score for your grade level (e.g., cut score of 201 for Grade 3 in Figure 6.7).

5. Define the lowest score and highest score for your class in the chart.

6. Add the chart title and any labels needed.

CHAPTER SEVEN:
THE BEAUTY OF DUAL LANGUAGE

REFLECTIONS FROM THE FIELD

Dr. Thomas and Dr. Collier's work has had a profound impact on the dual language program in our district. The English language learner population is here to stay. The question becomes how best to educate them. Their education needs to address academic development, language development, cognitive development, as well as social and cultural processes. The best program for the ultimate integration of and achievement in these areas is the dual language program. Ultimately, we are looking to close the achievement gap. There are no quick answers. As we expand our dual language program in the district from two to five schools, we use the work and words of Dr. Thomas and Dr. Collier as a guide. Their research helps us to clarify our vision as we expand our program, and we are grateful!

COLLEEN WAPOLE
IMMERSION COORDINATOR
PINELLAS COUNTY SCHOOLS, FLORIDA

CHAPTER SEVEN: THE BEAUTY OF DUAL LANGUAGE

We ascribe beauty to that which is simple; which has no superfluous parts; which exactly answers its end; which stands related to all things; which is the mean of many extremes.

RALPH WALDO EMERSON

First of all, what does it mean to be "elegant?" Roughly what I think this means is that a huge amount of structure is packaged in a small number of simple principles.

PETER WOIT

Mathematicians, physicists, and philosophers speak of beauty and elegance in scientific explanations that are simple but powerful. But do these concepts apply to dual language education? We believe that they do. Why is dual language so successful? What makes it work so well?

Theoretical foundations of dual language education

First, dual language education is consistent with well-founded theory from the fields of education, linguistics, and the social sciences. Researchers from all continents of the world have concluded that the research evidence is clear and consistent that schooling through two languages is very effective when well implemented (Bühmann & Trudell, 2008; Cummins, 2000b; García, Skutnabb-Kangas & Torres-Guzmán, 2006; Ouane & Glanz, 2011; Pacific Policy Research Center, 2010; Skutnabb-Kangas, Phillipson, Mohanty & Panda, 2009).

The research syntheses on which our Prism Model is based (Collier, 1995a, 1995b, 1995c; Collier & Thomas, 2007, 2009) provide an overview of the theoretical foundations on which dual language programs are grounded. The Prism Model focuses on the natural developmental processes in children that occur during the school years, identifying four interwoven dimensions that influence academic achievement. These are sociocultural (including emotional), linguistic, cognitive, and academic development. For children growing up in a bilingual environment, these four developmental processes must occur through both one's first and second languages in order for students to experience success in school. By multiplying four processes times two languages, this results in a total of eight dimensions to be addressed when educating bilingual learners. Some of the most important concepts to remember are as follows:

- Achievement gaps begin when the eight Prism dimensions (linguistic, academic, cognitive, and sociocultural development in both first and second languages) are not adequately addressed. Properly implemented dual language programs fully address all eight dimensions.

- Second language acquisition is a process that cannot be taught explicitly, but the new language is acquired by having meaningful experiences in that language that connect to what each student already knows. The dual language teachers facilitate this process, and student collaboration and interaction is crucial, using cooperative learning strategies.

- For English learners, first language schooling is necessary for full gap closure and accelerating academic achievement. The number of years of instruction through English learners' primary language is the most powerful predictor of long-term academic success in English. At least six years are required.

- Cognitive development is directly connected to first language development. To be in an additive bilingual context, children must receive nonstop cognitive development in their primary language, from birth through young adulthood, while developing their second language. Additive bilinguals may also develop cognitively in two languages from birth on, with both languages serving as their primary languages. Dual language programs are especially powerful in fostering cognitive development through both languages, making school an additive bilingual context for all students enrolled in dual language classes.

- Additive bilingualism leads to bilinguals' greater ability to solve problems; to be more creative; to be divergent, flexible, original thinkers; and to develop more metalinguistic awareness than monolinguals.

- Social and cultural support is crucial. Students need to feel safe and secure, respected and valued for their rich life experiences from other cultural contexts that they bring to the classroom. Dual language classes incorporate cross-cultural perspectives that affirm and value students' bilingual/bicultural identities.

- Dual language classes assist with "the collaborative creation of power within the classroom" (Cummins, 2009, p. 34), transforming minority-majority relations into equity for all.

Closing the achievement gap

In the political atmosphere of high-stakes testing emphasized over the past decade in the U.S., policy-makers have put much pressure on educators to follow students' progress and close the achievement gaps for all groups. Dual language education has been remarkably effective at doing this. Administrators and teachers of mature, well-implemented dual language programs have demonstrated consistent success year after year with students' high achievement in both languages, so that there is less anxiety about how students will do on the tests, and more focus on curricular innovation through the two languages. This is very similar to student progress, creativity, and accelerated learning in a gifted program.

The real achievement gap for English learners after two to three years of development of English as a second language is larger than most educators realize. At this point in their English language development, the true size of their achievement gap when tested in English is 1.0-1.5 (average 1.2) national standard deviations on a difficult norm-referenced test. This is equivalent to the difference between the 50th and 22nd percentiles. However, almost all state tests are easier than norm-referenced tests and thus show a smaller gap because of their ceiling effect that limits the scores of the most competent test-takers. Also, because many states set low passing scores, former English learners can often pass easier state tests with a score that is well below the state average for native English speakers. For these reasons, using state tests to assess the achievement gap often provides a falsely low assessment of the true size of the gap. English learners attending dual language programs fully close the gap and keep it closed, as measured by both the state tests and the more difficult norm-referenced tests. These more difficult tests are also of the same type as the measures used for entrance into university study (e.g., PSAT, SAT, ACT).

Furthermore, the first half of the achievement gap is much easier to close than the second half. Why? After mastering the easier curricular content and test items in the early years of instruction (and closing the first half of the achievement gap), English learners need substantial cognitive development to master the remaining difficult test items. In addition, they face still more challenging curricula and test items in late elementary and middle school, so that they can close the second half of the gap and perform at the same level as the native English speakers who have reached grade-level achievement. Typical transitional bilingual and ESL programs do not provide this necessary cognitive development, but dual language programs do.

A successful dual language experience in the elementary school years is key to full closure of the achievement gap, because this is when the achievement gap is easiest to close. English learners must make more than one year's progress each year in both L1 and L2 to eventually catch up to native English speakers, who are continuing to make one year's progress each year. English learners who have not reached grade-level achievement in at least one of their two languages by the end of elementary school will experience more difficulties at the secondary level. Gap closure is much more challenging in middle and high school because the curriculum and the tests become more complex and difficult with each successive grade level. For these reasons, programs that can close all of the achievement gap during the elementary years (i.e., dual language programs) are highly advantageous for English learners as compared to other programs that only close up to half of the full gap.

What is amazing is that dual language programs close the achievement gap not only for English learners but also for other groups as well. Latinos fluent in English, African Americans, and students of low socioeconomic status from all ethnic backgrounds have greatly improved their test scores within dual language classes, benefitting these groups more dramatically than other school reform models. Fully meeting the needs of historically underserved and low-scoring groups is an important reason to expand access to dual language classes for as many student groups as possible.

Additional positive outcomes in dual language education

Of course so much more happens in school than what can be measured on a test. Research studies and syntheses of research on dual language outcomes conducted by Lindholm-Leary (2001, 2009) and Thomas, Collier & Collier (2010) have identified many additional benefits from attending dual language classes. Dual language students have more favorable attitudes toward being bilingual and bicultural. They view fellow students who are different from themselves very positively. And they have high self-esteem and stronger clarity about their bicultural identity. Dual language students report high levels of satisfaction and enjoyment in dual language classes. Student engagement with instruction is higher in dual language classes. Student overall interest in school is higher in dual language programs. Student attendance is better in dual language programs. We also found that there are significantly fewer behavioral referrals experienced in dual language classes than in the English mainstream classes.

Figure 7.1 illustrates the influences these positive experiences may have on each other, in the form of positive feedback loops. Dual language programs result in improved student interest in school, increased cognitive stimulation, and increased student engagement with instruction, leading to higher student achievement. As students enjoy increasing success in school and become proud of their ability to speak, read, and write more than one language, their self-concept improves. This then influences their desire to attend classes regularly, and they become more engaged and confident learners, leading to higher achievement, which feeds back to improved student motivation and fewer disciplinary referrals. In turn, these factors increase student achievement and this influences all the primary and secondary factors just named, as illustrated in Figure 7.1. The process becomes self-reinforcing. The interactions among all these factors lead to even higher achievement in the long term.

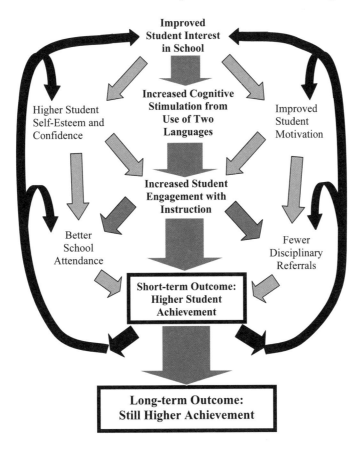

Figure 7.1

Positive Instructional Feedback Loops and
Their Effects on Dual Language (DL) Program Outcomes

DL programs have the largest program effect sizes (typically .15 to .25 national standard deviations per year) of all ELL program types. This instructional acceleration leads to higher-than-normal achievement for ELLs each year and allows them to outgain typical native English speakers for each year that they participate in the DL program.

But there's more – this process is self-reinforcing!

Improved
Student Interest
in School

Increased Cognitive
Stimulation from
Use of Two
Languages

Higher Student
Self-Esteem and
Confidence

Improved
Student
Motivation

Increased Student
Engagement with
Instruction

Better
School
Attendance

Fewer
Disciplinary
Referrals

**Short-term Outcome:
Higher Student
Achievement**

**Long-term Outcome:
Still Higher Achievement**

Copyright © 2004-2012, W.P. Thomas & V.P. Collier. All rights reserved.

Chapter Seven—The Beauty of Dual Language

Among the most dramatic outcomes of attending dual language classes is that all students acquire a new language at a deep level of academic proficiency. (See Cummins, 1981, 2000b for his theories regarding social and academic language.) This type of language learning is unlike foreign language classes that focus on an average of 45 minutes per day of listening, speaking, reading, writing, and studying the grammar patterns of the language, or foreign language classes in the elementary school that focus mainly on social and conversational language. In contrast, dual language classes use the new language through all subjects of the school curriculum, in a subconscious acquisition process that parallels the natural way that an infant acquires the first language (Bialystok, 1991, 2001; Dulay, Burt & Krashen, 1982; Tabors, 1997).

While attending the dual language classes, meaningful interaction in the new language over many years, as well as explicit studies about the language (as in a foreign language or language arts class), lead to the most profound levels of acquisition of the new language. The ultimate prize is graduating from high school with a biliteracy diploma that has prepared the students for oral and written uses of their two languages throughout their adult lives in both professional and personal contexts. And because the students started this process when they were only five years of age, they also speak the new language with native speaker pronunciation, something rarely achieved in foreign language classes taught at the secondary level.

Teacher creativity and curricular reform in dual language classes

Dual language classes are a natural setting for carefully planned experimentation in teaching (Reyes &Kleyn, 2010). The mix of students with many different needs in each class leads to differentiated instruction as a model implemented with the whole class, instead of having specialists pulling students out of the class. This is not remedial or programmed instruction. Instead the class is a vehicle for instructional practices that have known power, such as cooperative learning and GLAD (Guided Language Acquisition Design). Teaching through the two languages becomes accelerated and gifted instruction for English learners, as well as for native English speakers, leading to all dual language students' potential giftedness, expressed through increased creativity and problem-solving abilities. English learners need cognitively stimulating, comprehensible, exciting instruction that connects to their life experiences, whereas "watered down" and "scripted" instruction may produce short-term achievement gains but not sustained, long-term gains (Freeman, 2004).

Dual language programs also provide the infrastructure for teachers to be innovative, through ongoing staff development, instructional coaching, team mentoring, and structured planning time for partner teachers to confer together.

Program coordinators and biliteracy coaches can work with the bilingual teachers to choose and create developmentally appropriate and challenging curricular materials in the two languages. Training for dual language teachers includes many strategies for making content comprehensible through the second language and dual language classes include more inquiry, more collaboration, and more project-based learning with peers (Cloud, Genesee & Hamayan, 2000; Freeman, Freeman & Mercuri, 2005). Because half of the students in each two-way class are still acquiring the instructional language, these strategies are crucial, and they lead to teaching styles that facilitate accelerated learning in both languages. (See many dual language teaching strategies, including GLAD teaching practices, described in detail in the quarterly publication *Soleado*, produced by Dual Language Education of New Mexico—*www.dlenm.org*.)

Furthermore, these types of teaching styles especially benefit all students who might struggle in a traditional English mainstream classroom. This may be one of the clues to explaining the high achievement of African American students, language minority students, and students of low socioeconomic background when enrolled in dual language classes. The second language teaching strategies help everyone in the class, by beginning a lesson with experiences that connect to what the students already know, developing new vocabulary and language that will be used in the lesson, and then moving into the content itself. In contrast, teachers in mainstream English classes often assume that students already know the language and thus content typically comes first, followed by modifications. In dual language classes, second language teaching strategies benefit all students.

And then there's the concept of more, more, more—proposed by politicians and laypersons. Why not more years of English-only instruction, more drills on phonics and grammar points, more memorizing of vocabulary, more homework, more instructional time, a longer school year? Do these really work?

Dual language classroom experiences imply that **more is not always better!** Focusing on interesting and comprehensible instruction for an optimal amount of time is a much more efficient and productive strategy. The relationship between inputs (e.g., time-on-task) and outputs (achievement) may appear to be a straight-line relationship at first, but it is really quadratic. As can be seen in Figure 7.2, a quadratic relationship is represented by an inverted-U-shape with a "maximum effect point" or "saturation point." After the maximum effect point is reached, achievement stops increasing and more inputs lead to lower outputs, not higher. When students have reached their saturation point, they'll stare out the window or fidget or misbehave. In the early stages of language learning, the saturation point can come pretty quickly. So what do dual language classes do? At the appropriate time in the instruction, teachers and students switch to the other language and continue

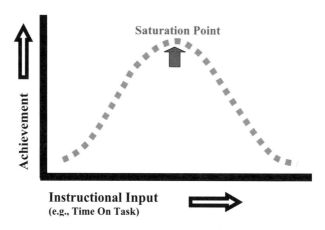

Figure 7.2

More Is Not Always Better!
Important Non-Linear Relationships
Between Program Inputs and Student Achievement

Saturation Point

Achievement

Instructional Input
(e.g., Time On Task)

Student achievement initially increases with more instructional inputs, but only to a point! After that point is reached, more instructional inputs lead to lower achievement, not higher. The lesson is: "More input is not necessarily or always better! (As in the invalid assertion: "All they need is more English.")

Copyright © 2004-2012, W.P. Thomas & V.P. Collier. All rights reserved.

continue learning in that language. This does not mean translation or code-switching, but following the dual language guidelines established for separation of the two languages (as discussed in Chapter 3). Switching to the other language often has the effect of renewing student engagement with learning. It also resets the saturation point to a higher level that allows increased educational productivity and higher student achievement.

A related concept is something we hear from many teachers who have not been trained in dual language methodology: "If we're going to test in English, we should teach in English." At first glance, this may seem like common sense, but yielding to pressure to teach more in English is a serious mistake. What this really means is: "If we're going to test them in their weaker language for test validity, we should teach them in their less efficient language for learning." This makes little sense psychometrically or educationally.

Here's a different perspective on this issue, seen from a bilingual's point of view. First, dual language teachers know that the language of testing should be the language that yields the most accurate and valid achievement score, reflecting what the student actually knows, in any language. Therefore, if the state test is offered in the students' primary language, that should be the measure chosen at third grade level (the typical first year of state testing). Second, using students' first language (typically more efficient for learning than second language) in instruction, and using English as well for a portion of the academic year, leads to more comprehensible instruction, better achievement, and higher test scores, even when the end-of-year test is administered in English. As long as students have mastered enough English to understand and respond to the test items, their increased understanding of content presented in their first language will lead to higher scores in English than in all-English instruction.

As an example, one of our school district research sites found that newly arriving high school immigrants not yet proficient in English were having a very difficult time passing the state test on the course titled Government, required for graduation from high school. One year the bilingual teachers chose to offer this course in Vietnamese and Spanish (the two largest demographic groups among new arrivals). At the end of the year, these ESL students took the state test in English and scored higher than the native English speakers taking the same test. When the course was taught in these students' primary language, the material became more meaningful and comprehensible to them than in their second language (English), illustrating that more English does not mean higher test scores in English.

Variability in dual language outcomes: Is your program well implemented?

Dual language programs have the potential to raise student achievement to the highest levels we have seen in any school innovation. Well-implemented two-way programs have almost twice the effect size of traditional bilingual/ESL programs for English learners (Collier & Thomas, 2009). But for this type of enrichment and acceleration to happen, fidelity to the non-negotiable and essential components of well-implemented dual language education (as described in Chapters 1-4 of this book) really matters!

Since dual language education is potentially the most powerful program of all, it is also the program most strongly affected by how well it is implemented. Therefore, it is very important that educators pay close attention to full and faithful implementation of dual language education, according to research-based guidelines. Variations in implementation can have a substantial negative or positive effect on student outcomes.

Figure 7.3 illustrates the range of variability that we have seen in English learners' achievement within dual language programs on the reading measure in English. The green and blue lines come from Figure 6.1 in the last chapter. These two lines represent the average English learner achievement of all our dual language studies combined together. Reaching the 61st NCE by Grade 11 are former English learners who attended two-way dual language classes. At the 52nd NCE by Grade 11 are former English learners who attended one-way dual language classes.

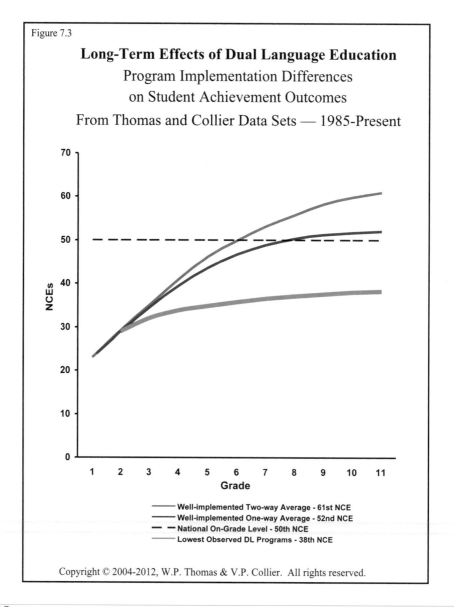

Figure 7.3

Long-Term Effects of Dual Language Education

Program Implementation Differences
on Student Achievement Outcomes

From Thomas and Collier Data Sets — 1985-Present

——— Well-implemented Two-way Average - 61st NCE
——— Well-implemented One-way Average - 52nd NCE
– – National On-Grade Level - 50th NCE
——— Lowest Observed DL Programs - 38th NCE

Copyright © 2004-2012, W.P. Thomas & V.P. Collier. All rights reserved.

The red line represents the lowest English learner achievement that we have seen in classes that were labeled dual language. These were two-way 50:50 Spanish-English programs, in which throughout their elementary school years, the native English speakers attended their own classes in English for half of the day while the English learners received intensive ESL lessons. The two groups worked together only during the Spanish instructional time. Separation of the two groups during the English instructional time led to approximately the same achievement levels for the English learners as that of a well-implemented transitional bilingual education program, with only half of their gap in English closed (see Figure 6.1; Thomas & Collier, 1997).

Integration is important. English learners need to be welcomed and valued in a class that includes native English speakers and language minority students. To be faithful to implementation practices that work, dual language classes keep students together for all instruction, so that they can wrestle cognitively with the concepts together, providing language modeling for each other, and respecting and valuing what each student offers. They also serve as important peer tutors for each other, when the instruction is conducted in each language. **By keeping the students together and intentionally building a classroom and school community that respects and values all students, social and cultural relationships are transformed.**

Connecting to the school community

Another crucial component of dual language schooling that makes this program so successful is the close school-community partnership that develops as the school reaches out to parents and community. Parents who speak the partner language feel genuinely welcome in the bilingual/multicultural school. Home-school partnerships often start with the relationship with the bilingual teachers, discussing homework and ways that parents can support their children's academic success.

Quite often in our research sites, we find that the most successful dual language schools tend to go far beyond this initial step, and as needed, to provide services that assist families with their needs. Examples are parent literacy projects, parenting classes, bilingual family health services, multicultural celebrations, and parents sharing their "funds of knowledge" (Moll, Vélez-Ibáñez, Greenberg & Rivera, 1990) with students and the school community. As dual language parents become advocates for the school, they assist with community meetings that explain the program to new parents and that meet the needs of the newly arriving families. Community advocacy may include business partners who donate funds for needed school technology and materials in the partner language. Partnerships can even extend to sister schools in other countries to exchange visits and curricular explorations via Internet.

Summary

We began this chapter by asking what makes dual language work so well. In physics, an elegant scientific theory is simple and powerful. That's the beauty of it. This educational program has a simple, well-defined theory, with measurable variables and outcomes that respond to inputs. The high outcomes of dual language schooling are consistent with the outcomes that theory and research-based practice would predict for its program components and instructional strategies when well implemented. The program is maximally effective in the early years of school, when the gap is easiest to close, and thus it puts students in a better position for achieving on grade level in the middle and high school years, when the cognitive demand of instruction is high.

Dual language education is also politically attractive, with majority support. Many of the voices in opposition to traditional bilingual education are supportive of this particular model of bilingual schooling. Designed for all students, rather than being divisive and isolating, this program is integrative and inclusive. All student groups—English learners, Hispanic Americans, Asian Americans, African Americans, Caucasian Americans, students of low income background, and students with exceptionalities—benefit greatly from dual language classes. Because dual language is a vehicle for school reform, it meets the needs of students, educators, and the whole community.

Creating and sustaining a good dual language school requires substantial planning, sustained focus on core concepts, and a great deal of collaborative work among teachers, administrators, and parents. When all of these are well carried out, the results can be truly remarkable in transforming and greatly improving the quality of schooling that all students receive. We must remind ourselves that we are educating our students to be the adults who will run our countries and our world in the 2030s and beyond. We must also realize that our efforts to transform their education through dual language schooling are critically important to maximize our own future quality of life in our rapidly transforming world.

APPENDIX A: TABLE OF FIGURES

References

Andersson, T., & Boyer, M. (Eds.). (1978). *Bilingual schooling in the United States* (2nd ed.). Austin, TX: National Educational Laboratory Publishers.

Baker, C. (2011). *Foundations of bilingual education and bilingualism* (5th ed.). Bristol, UK: Multilingual Matters.

Baker, C., & Hornberger, N.H. (Eds.). (2001). *An introductory reader to the writings of Jim Cummins*. Bristol, UK: Multilingual Matters.

Baker, C., & Prys-Jones, S. (1998). *Encyclopedia of bilingualism and bilingual education*. Bristol, UK: Multilingual Matters.

Benson, C. (2004). *The importance of mother tongue-based schooling for educational quality*. Paper commissioned for the *Education for All Global Monitoring Report 2005, The Quality Imperative*, UNESCO. Stockholm: Centre for Research on Bilingualism, Stockholm University. *http://unesdoc.unesco.org/images/0014/001466/146632e.pdf*

Bialystok, E. (Ed.). (1991). *Language processing in bilingual children*. Cambridge: Cambridge University Press.

Bialystok, E. (2001). *Bilingualism in development: Language, literacy, and cognition*. Cambridge: Cambridge University Press.

Bolton, L., & Baxter, S. (Eds.). (2011). *Helpdesk report: Language of instruction*. London: Human Development Resource Centre, UK Department for International Development. *http://hdrc.dfid.gov.uk/wp-content/uploads/2012/05/Language-of-Instruction-June-2011.pdf*

Bruck, M. (1982). Language disabled children: Performance in an additive bilingual education program. *Applied Psycholinguistics, 3,* 45-60.

Bühmann, D., & Trudell, B. (2008). *Mother tongue matters: Local language as a key to effective learning*. Paris: UNESCO. *http://unesdoc.unesco.org/images/0016/001611/161121e.pdf*

Castellanos, D. (1983). *The best of two worlds: Bilingual-bicultural education in the U.S.* Trenton, NJ: New Jersey State Department of Education.

Christian, D., & Genesee, F. (Eds.). (2001). *Bilingual education*. Alexandria, VA: Teachers of English to Speakers of Other Languages.

Cloud, N., Genesee, F., & Hamayan, E. (2000). *Dual language instruction: A hand-book for enriched education.* Boston, MA: Heinle & Heinle.

Cohen, A.D. (1976). The case for partial or total immersion education. In A. Simoes, Jr. (Ed.), *The bilingual child* (pp. 65-89). New York: Academic Press.

Coleman, H. (2007). *Language and development: Africa and beyond.* Addis Ababa, Ethiopia: British Council Ethiopia. *http://englishagenda.britishcouncil.org/sites/ec/files/language%20&%20Development%20Africa%20and%20Beyond.pdf*

Collier, V.P. (1992). A synthesis of studies examining long-term language minority student data on academic achievement. *Bilingual Research Journal, 16*(1-2), 187-212. (See *http://www.thomasandcollier.com –Research links.*)

Collier, V.P. (1995a). *Acquiring a second language for school.* Washington, DC: National Clearinghouse for English Language Acquisition. (See *http://www.thomasand-collier.com – Research links.*)

Collier, V.P. (1995b). *Promoting academic success for ESL students: Understanding second language acquisition for school.* Elizabeth, NJ: New Jersey Teachers of English to Speakers of Other Languages-Bilingual Educators.

Collier, V.P. (1995c). Second language acquisition for school: Academic, cognitive, sociocultural, and linguistic processes. In J.E. Alatis et al. (Eds.). *Georgetown University Round Table on Languages and Linguistics 1995* (pp. 311-327). Washington, DC: Georgetown University Press. (See *http://www.thomasand-collier.com – Research links.*)

Collier, V.P., & Thomas, W.P. (2007). Predicting second language academic success in English using the Prism Model. In J. Cummins & C. Davison (Eds.), *International handbook of English language teaching, Part 1* (pp. 333-348). New York: Springer.

Collier, V.P., & Thomas, W.P. (2009). *Educating English learners for a transformed world.* Albuquerque, NM: Dual Language Education of New Mexico-Fuente Press. *http://www.dlenm.org*

Crawford, J. (1999). *Bilingual education: History, politics, theory, and practice* (4th ed.). Los Angeles: Bilingual Educational Services.

Cummins, J. (1981). The role of primary language development in promoting educational success for language minority students. In California State Department of Education (Ed.), *Schooling and language minority students: A theoretical framework.* Los Angeles: California State University; Evaluation, Dissemination, and Assessment Center.

Cummins, J. (1991). Interdependence of first- and second-language proficiency in bilingual children. In E. Bialystok (Ed.), *Language processing in bilingual children* (pp. 70-89). Cambridge: Cambridge University Press.

Cummins, J. (2000a). Biliteracy, empowerment, and transformative pedagogy. In J.V. Tinajero & R.A. DeVillar (Eds.), *The power of two languages 2000: Effective dual-language use across the curriculum* (pp. 9-19). New York: McGraw-Hill.

Cummins, J. (2000b). *Language, power and pedagogy: Bilingual children in the crossfire.* Bristol, UK: Multilingual Matters.

Cummins, J. (2008). Teaching for transfer: Challenging the two solitudes assumption in bilingual education. In J. Cummins & N.H. Hornberger (Eds.), *Encyclopedia of Language and Education: Vol. 5, Bilingual Education* (2nd ed., pp. 65-76). New York: Springer.

Cummins, J. (2009). Fundamental psycholinguistic and sociological principles underlying educational success for linguistic minority students. In T. Skutnabb-Kangas, R. Phillipson, A.K. Mohanty & M. Panda (Eds.), *Social justice through multilingual education* (pp. 19-35). Bristol, UK: Multilingual Matters.

Cummins, J., & Hornberger, N.H. (Eds.). (2008). *Encyclopedia of Language and Education. Vol. 5, Bilingual Education* (2nd ed.). New York: Springer.

Cummins, J., & Swain, M. (1986). *Bilingualism in education.* New York: Longman.

de Jong, E.J. (2011). *Foundations for multilingualism in education: From principles to practice.* Philadelphia: Caslon.

Díaz, R.M., & Klingler, C. (1991). Towards an explanatory model of the interaction between bilingualism and cognitive development. In E. Bialystok (Ed.), *Language processing in bilingual children* (pp. 167-192). Cambridge: Cambridge University Press.

Dolson, D. (1985). Bilingualism and scholastic performance: The literature revisited. *NABE Journal, 10*(1), 1-35. (ERIC Document Reproduction Service No. EJ 367 966 and ED 291 257)

Dulay, H., Burt, M., & Krashen, S. (1982). *Language two.* New York: Oxford University Press.

Dutcher, N. (2001). *The use of first and second languages in education: A review of international experience* (2nd ed.). Washington, DC: Center for Applied Linguistics. *http://www.wds.worldbank.org/servlet/WDSContentServer/WDSP/IB/2000/02/24/000094946_99031910564840/Rendered/PDF/multi_page.pdf*

Epstein, N. (1977). *Language, ethnicity, and the schools: Policy alternatives for bilingual-bicultural education.* Washington, DC: Institute for Educational Leadership, George Washington University.

Escamilla, K. (2000). Teaching literacy in Spanish. In J.V. Tinajero & R.A. DeVillar (Eds.), *The power of two languages 2000: Effective dual-language use across the curriculum* (pp. 126-141). New York: McGraw-Hill.

Fishman, J. (1976). *Bilingual education: An international sociological perspective.* New York: Newbury House.

Francis, N., & Reyhner, J. (2002). *Language and literacy teaching for indigenous education: A bilingual approach.* Bristol, UK: Multilingual Matters.

Freeman, R. (2004). *Building on community bilingualism: Promoting multilingualism through schooling.* Philadelphia: Caslon.

Freeman, Y.S., & Freeman, D.E. (2006). *Teaching reading and writing in Spanish and English in bilingual and dual language classrooms* (2nd ed.). Portsmouth, NH: Heinemann.

Freeman, Y.S., Freeman, D.E., & Mercuri, S.P. (2005). *Dual language essentials for teachers and administrators.* Portsmouth, NH: Heinemann.

Gándara, P., & Hopkins, M. (Eds.). (2010). *Forbidden language: English learners and restrictive language policies.* New York: Teachers College Press.

García, O., Skuttnabb-Kangas, T., & Torres-Guzmán, M.E. (Eds.). (2006). *Imagining multilingual schools: Languages in education and globalization.* Bristol, UK: Multilingual Matters.

Genesee, F. (1987). *Learning through two languages: Studies of immersion and bilingual education.* New York: Newbury House.

Genesee, F. (2007). French immersion and at-risk students: A review of research findings. *Canadian Modern Language Review, 63,* 655-688. (ERIC Document Reproduction Service No. EJ 784 166)

Genesee, F., Paradis, J., & Crago, M.B. (2004). *Dual language development and disorders: A handbook on bilingualism and second language learning.* Baltimore: Paul H. Brookes Publishing.

Goldenberg, C. (2000). Promoting early literacy development among Spanish-speaking children: Lessons from two studies. In J.V. Tinajero & R.A. DeVillar (Eds.), *The power of two languages 2000: Effective dual-language use across the curriculum* (pp. 83-101). New York: McGraw-Hill.

Goldenberg, C. (2008). Teaching English language learners: What the research does—and does not—say. *American Educator, 32*(2), 8-23, 42-44. *http://www.aft.org/pubs-reports/american_educator/issues/summer08/goldenberg.pdf*

Greene, J. (1998). *A meta-analysis of the effectiveness of bilingual education.* Austin, TX: Tomas Rivera Policy Institute, University of Texas-Austin. *http://www.languagepolicy.net/archives/greene.htm*

Groff, C. (2005). Evaluations of bilingual and mother-tongue programs: Measures of success and means of measurement. *Working Papers in Educational Linguistics, 20*(2), 19-39. *http://www.gse.upenn.edu/sites/gse.upenn.edu.wpel/files/archives/v20/v20n2_Groff.pdf*

Hélot, C., & de Mejía, A. (2008). *Forging multilingual spaces: Integrated perspectives on majority and minority bilingual education.* Bristol, UK: Multilingual Matters.

Howard, E.R., Christian, D., & Genesee, F. (2003). The development of bilingualism and biliteracy from Grade 3 to 5: A summary of findings from the CAL/CREDE study of two-way immersion education, *CREDE Research Report 12.* Santa Cruz, CA, and Washington, DC: Center for Research on Education, Diversity & Excellence.

Klaus, D. (2003). The use of indigenous languages in early basic education in Papua New Guinea: A model for elsewhere? *Language and Education, 17*(2), 105-111. *http://www.pnglanguages.org/asia/ldc/parallel_papers/david_klaus.pdf*

Kloss, H. (1998). *The American bilingual tradition.* McHenry, IL: Center for Applied Linguistics/Delta Systems.

Krashen, S., & Biber, D. (1988). *On course: Bilingual education's success in California.* Sacramento, CA: California Association for Bilingual Education.

Lachance, J., & Marino, J. (2012). English learners in North Carolina: A unique response. *NABE Perspectives, 34*(3), 16-22. *http://www.nabe.org/Resources/Documents/NABE%20Perspectives/NN_34n3_Mar_Apr2012.pdf*

Lambert, W.E. (1975). Culture and language as factors in learning and education. In A. Wolfgang (Ed.), *Education of immigrant students.* Toronto: Ontario Institute for Studies in Education.

Lambert, W.E. (1984). An overview of issues in immersion education. In *Studies on immersion education: A collection for United States educators* (pp. 8-30). Sacramento, CA: California Department of Education.

Lau v. Nichols, 414 U.S. 563 (1974).

Legarreta, D. (1979). The effects of program models on language acquisition by Spanish-speaking children. *TESOL Quarterly, 13,* 521-534.

Legarreta, D. (1981). Effective use of the primary language in the classroom. In *Schooling and language minority students* (pp. 83-116). Sacramento, CA: California Department of Education.

Leibowitz, A.H. (1980). *The Bilingual Education Act: A legislative analysis.* Washington, DC: National Clearinghouse for English Language Acquisition. (ERIC Document Reproduction Service No. 192 614)

Lindholm-Leary, K. (1990). Bilingual immersion education: Criteria for program development. In A.M. Padilla, H.H. Fairchild, & C.M. Valadez (Eds.), *Bilingual education: Issues and strategies* (pp. 91-105). Newbury Park, CA: SAGE.

Lindholm-Leary, K. (2001). *Dual language education.* Bristol, UK: Multilingual Matters.

Lindholm-Leary, K. (2009). *Effective features of dual language education programs: A review of research and best practices.* Albuquerque, NM: Dual Language Education of New Mexico. *http://www.dlenm.org/index.php?option=com_content&view=article&id=126:programmatic-resources&catid=51:general&Itemid=5*

Lindholm-Leary, K., & Borsato, G. (2006). Academic achievement. In F. Genesee, K. Lindholm-Leary, W. Saunders, & D. Christian (Eds.), *Educating English language learners: A synthesis of research evidence* (pp. 176-222). New York: Cambridge University Press.

Lindholm-Leary, K., & Genesee, F. (2010). Alternative educational programs for English learners. In *Improving Education for English Learners: Research-based approaches* (pp. 323-382). Sacramento, CA: California Department of Education.

Lindholm-Leary, K., & Howard, E. (2008). Language and academic achievement in two-way immersion programs. In T. Fortune & D. Tedick (Eds.), *Pathways to bilingualism: Evolving perspectives on immersion education.* Bristol, UK: Multilingual Matters.

Lyons, J. (1990). The past and future directions of federal bilingual-education policy. In C.B. Cazden & C.E. Snow (Eds.)., *The Annals of the American Academy of Political and Social Science*, Vol. 508 (pp. 66-80). Newbury Park, CA: Sage.

Mackey, W.F., & Beebe, V.N. (1977). *Bilingual schools for a bicultural community: Miami's adaptation to the Cuban refugees.* New York: Newbury House.

Magga, O.H., Nicolaisen, I., Trask, M., Skutnabb-Kangas, T., & Dunbar, R. (2005). *Indigenous children's education and indigenous languages.* Expert paper written for the United Nations Permanent Forum on Indigenous Issues. *http://www.tove-skutnabb-kangas.org/pdf/PFII_Expert_paper_1_Education_final.pdf*

Malone, S. (2004, January). Education for multilingualism and multi-literacy in ethnic minority communities: The situation in Asia. *Asian/Pacific Book Development, 34*(2). *http://www.sil.org/asia/ldc/plenary_papers/susan_malone.pdf*

May, S., & Hill, R. (2005). Maori-medium education: Current issues and challenges. *International Journal of Bilingual education and Bilingualism, 8*(5), 377-403. *http://researchcommons.waikato.ac.nz/handle/10289/529*

May, S., Hill, R., & Tiakiwai, S. (2004). *Bilingual/immersion education: Indicators of good practice: Final report to the Ministry of Education.* Wellington, New Zealand: Ministry of Education. *http://www.educationcounts.govt.nz/publications/schooling/5079*

Milk, R. (1986). The issue of language separation in bilingual methodology. In E. García & B. Flores (Eds.), *Language and literacy research in bilingual education* (pp. 67-86). Tempe, AZ: Center for Bilingual Education, Arizona State University.

Moll, L.C., Vélez-Ibáñez, C., Greenberg, J., & Rivera, C. (1990). *Community knowledge and classroom practice: Combining resources for literacy instruction.* Arlington, VA: Development Associates.

Ouane, A., & Glanz, C. (Eds.). (2011). *Optimising learning, education and publishing in Africa: The language factor: A review and analysis of theory and practice in mother-tongue and bilingual education in sub-Saharan Africa.* Hamburg, Germany, and Tunis Belvédère, Tunisia: UNESCO Institute for Lifelong Learning and Association for the Development of Education in Africa. *http://unesdoc.unesco.org/images/0021/002126/212602e.pdf*

Ovando, C.J., Combs, M.C., & Collier, V.P. (2006). *Bilingual and ESL classrooms: Teaching in multicultural contexts* (4th ed.). New York: McGraw-Hill.

Pacific Policy Research Center. (2010). *Successful bilingual and immersion education models/programs.* Honolulu: Kamehameha Schools, Research & Evaluation Division. *http://www.ksbe.edu/spi/PDFS/Bilingual%20Immersion%20full.pdf*

Ramírez, J.D.(1992). Executive summary. *Bilingual Research Journal, 16*(1-2), 1-62.

Reyes, S.A., & Kleyn, T. (2010). *Teaching in two languages: A guide for K-12 bilingual educators.* Thousand Oaks, CA: Corwin.

Rogers, D. (2009). Meeting the challenge—Maintaining an effective dual language program. *Soleado: Promising Practices from the Field, 1*(4), 1, 10. *http://www.soleado.dlenm.org.*

Rolstad, K., Mahoney, K., & Glass, G.V. (2005). The big picture: A meta-analysis of program effectiveness research on English language learners. *Educational Policy, 19*(4), 572-594. *http://www.educationjustice.org/assets/files/pdf/Resources/Policy/Programs%20That%20Work/The%20big%20picture.pdf*

Romero, M.E. (2007). *Language socialization of Pueblo Indian children.* Paper presented at the Reclaiming Our Children through Language: A Native Language Symposium. Albuquerque, NM: University of New Mexico.

Rosier, P., & Holm, W. (1980). *The Rock Point experience: A longitudinal study of a Navajo school program.* Washington, DC: Center for Applied Linguistics. (ERIC Document Reproduction Service No. ED 195 363)

Sizemore, C. (2011). Planning for secondary dual language—Asking the critical questions. *Soleado: Promising Practices from the Field, 3*(3), 2-3. *http://www.soleado.dlenm.org.*

Skutnabb-Kangas, T. (1979). *Language in the process of cultural assimilation and structural incorporation of linguistic minorities.* Washington, DC: National Clearinghouse for Bilingual Education.

Skutnabb-Kangas, T., Phillipson, R., Mohanty, A.K., & Panda, M. (Eds.). (2009). *Social justice through multilingual education.* Bristol, UK: Multilingual Matters.

Soltero, S.W. (2004). *Dual language: Teaching and learning in two languages.* Boston: Pearson.

Spolsky, B., & Cooper, R. (Eds.). (1977). *Frontiers of bilingual education.* New York: Newbury House.

Stern, H.H. (Ed.). (1963). *Foreign languages in primary education: The teaching of foreign or second languages to younger children.* Hamburg: International Studies in Education, UNESCO Institute for Education. *http://unesdoc. unesco.org/images/0013/001314/131496eo.pdf*

Swain, M., & Lapkin, S. (1981). *Bilingual education in Ontario: A decade of research.* Toronto: Ontario Institute for Studies in Education.

Swain, M., & Lapkin, S. (1982). *Evaluating bilingual education: A Canadian case study.* Bristol, UK: Multilingual Matters.

Tabors, P.O. (1997). *One child, two languages: A guide for preschool educators of children learning English as a second language.* Baltimore: Paul H.Brookes.

Thomas, W.P., & Collier, V.P. (1997). *School effectiveness for language minority students.* Washington, DC: National Clearinghouse for English Language Acquisition. (See *http://www.thomasandcollier.com –Research links.*)

Thomas, W.P., & Collier, V.P. (2002). *A national study of school effectiveness for language minority students' long-term academic achievement.* Santa Cruz, CA: Center for Research on Education, Diversity and Excellence, University of California-Santa Cruz. (See *http://www.thomasandcollier.com –Research links.*)

Thomas, W.P., & Collier, V.P. (2009). *English learners in North Carolina, 2009.* Fairfax, VA: George Mason University. A research report provided to the North Carolina Department of Public Instruction. *http://www.esl.ncwiseowl.org/resources/dual_language/*

Thomas, W.P., Collier, V.P., & Abbott, M. (1993). Academic achievement through Japanese, Spanish, or French: The first two years of partial immersion. *Modern Language Journal, 77*, 170-179. (See *http://www.thomasandcollier. com –Research links.)*

Thomas, W.P., Collier, V.P., & Collier, K. (2010). *English learners in North Carolina, 2010.* Fairfax, VA: George Mason University. A research report provided to the North Carolina Department of Public Instruction. *http:// www.esl.ncwiseowl.org/resources/dual_language/*

Thonis, E. (1994). Reading instruction for language minority students. In C.F. Leyba (Ed.), *Schooling and language minority students* (2nd ed., pp. 165-202). Los Angeles: Evaluation, Dissemination and Assessment Center, California State University, Los Angeles.

Tokuhama-Espinosa, T. (2003). *The multilingual mind.* Santa Barbara, CA: Praeger.

Troike, R. (1978). Research evidence for the effectiveness of bilingual education. *National Association for Bilingual Education Journal, 3*, 13-24. (ERIC Document Reproduction Service No. ED 159 900)

Tucker, G.R. (1999). A global perspective on bilingualism and bilingual education. *ERIC Digest.* Washington, DC: ERIC Clearinghouse on Languages and Linguistics, Center for Applied Linguistics. *http://www.cal.org/resources/ digest/digest_pdfs/9904-tucker-globalBE.pdf*

UNESCO. (1953). *The use of vernacular languages in education.* Monographs on Fundamental Education, No. 8. Paris: UNESCO. *http://unesdoc.unesco. org/images/0000/000028/002897eb.pdf*

Willig, A.C. (1985). A meta-analysis of selected studies on the effectiveness of bilingual education. *Review of Educational Research 55*(3), 269-317. (ERIC Document Reproduction Service No. EJ 324 690)

INDEX

About the Photographs

For the photographs in this book, DLeNM extends special thanks to:

- Mary Jean H. López for the photo of the authors;

- Moisés González for design of the cover image; and for the photos used to create the cover image, thanks to:

    - Albuquerque High School Alumni Association and the 1955 Student Affairs Committee;

    - Mishelle Jurado, Albuquerque High School teacher and sponsor of *Mentes Abiertas*... and to the dual language students in the organization;

- those schools and organizations whose students' faces begin each chapter:

    Cien Aguas International School, Eubank Elementary School, Wherry Elementary School, and Truman Middle School in Albuquerque; and the Student Leadership Institute, La Cosecha 2011.

About the Authors

Professors Wayne Thomas and Virginia Collier are internationally known for their research on long-term school effectiveness for linguistically and culturally diverse students. Dr. Thomas is a professor emeritus of evaluation and research methodology and Dr. Collier is a professor emerita of bilingual/multicultural/ESL education, both at George Mason University. This is  their second title in a series published by DLeNM and Fuente Press, following *Educating English Learners for a Transformed World*. For other publications by Dr. Thomas and Dr. Collier, please visit their website at *www.thomasandcollier.com*.

DLeNM is grateful to Starline Printing in Albuquerque
for their expertise and support in publishing
Dual Language Education for a Transformed World.